Plato

The Sophistes of Plato

A Dialogue on True and False Teaching

Plato

The Sophistes of Plato
A Dialogue on True and False Teaching

ISBN/EAN: 9783337003159

Printed in Europe, USA, Canada, Australia, Japan

Cover: Foto ©Thomas Meinert / pixelio.de

More available books at **www.hansebooks.com**

THE

SOPHISTES OF PLATO:

A DIALOGUE

ON TRUE AND FALSE TEACHING.

TRANSLATED, WITH

EXPLANATORY NOTES, AND AN INTRODUCTION

ON

ANCIENT AND MODERN SOPHISTRY.

BY

R. W. MACKAY, M.A.,

AUTHOR OF "THE PROGRESS OF THE INTELLECT;" "THE TUBINGEN SCHOOL
AND ITS ANTECEDENTS," ETC.

WILLIAMS AND NORGATE,
14, HENRIETTA STREET, COVENT GARDEN, LONDON:
AND 20, SOUTH FREDERICK STREET, EDINBURGH.

1868.

CONTENTS OF INTRODUCTION.

Two kinds of Education—Mr. Grote's so-called "German fiend" Die Sophistik — Its Existence and Connotation — Its Connection with the Political and Intellectual State of Athens—Speculative Theories of the Sophists; Perverse Applications of them by the Eristici—Philosophical Disparagement of Sophistical Culture Justified — Immoral Teaching of the Sophists—Teaching for Pay—Teaching to Please—Instances of Modern Sophistry—Tendency of Party or Class "Unionism" to Distort the Notion of Right and Wrong—Mr. Lowe's Recent Education Speech—The Objects of Education—The Sophist and the Martyr.

CORRECTIONS AND OMISSIONS.

Page 72, line 1. Literally, " more moderate than that of ordinary Eristic cavillers,"—or "than that of the generality of those devoting themselves to the business of controversy."

P. 81, l. 6. For *have* read *had*.

After l. 8, insert—

THEÆT.—Yes.

STRANG.—And now in regard to the Sophist; shall we assume him to be an ignoramus, or one really and truly a Sophist?

P. 88, l. 12 from below. "But the artificial kind, which embarks in general and systematic controversies on the essential nature of justice, injustice, and all other things, do we not usually call this the ' Eristic' or wrangling art ?"

L. 5 from below insert—

STRANG.—Let us now try to find a suitable name for each.

THEÆT.—We must do so.

P. 105, l. 14. For *is* read *was*.

P. 113, l. 1 from below, in the note. For *belongs* read *belong*.

POSTSCRIPT.

The following are extracts from the *Times* report of another speech on education just made by Mr. Lowe (Jan. 24th, 1868), affording additional proof that politicians, whether lay or ecclesiastical, are by no means the most reliable authorities on the subject :

"At a time when there was really nothing to learn or know, a number of foundations, which have continued to the present day unaltered, were made for teaching Latin and Greek."

As if Latin and Greek were mere empty forms of language, having no solid intellectual and moral contents ;—as if all modern culture were not based upon the old culture, and properly so !

"Latin and Greek, though not a bad education, are not the best; for the upper classes themselves, who *enjoy its advantages*, do not think it the best." "We have got to the end of our study of the dead languages."

Indeed ! Why, then, speak of it as a mere matter of grammar and dictionary, and recommend German as "a key to the more complete study of classical antiquity ?"

"Better to teach what is true, than what is demonstratively true."

But he had before complained that the habit of

taking things for granted is not a good one, and proceeds to recommend mathematics as inuring the mind to reason out its own conclusions.

"The processes of nature contemplated by physical science are far superior to those *mere works of man*, which we call literature, and history, and the actions of mankind."

As if oxygen, hydrogen, pneumatics, etc., were to be considered the sole or the chief illustrations of the divine laws and operations, and not the actions and eventualities of man!

Mr. Lowe emphatically disclaims history and moral philosophy as means of education, because the one is uncertain in its facts, the other in its theory. And yet history contains the record of nature's infallible judgments on the past, while moral philosophy offers the only means of bettering the humanity of the future!

"Don't cram a boy with stupid books; give him the most amusing French novel that can be found; a story that will give him some little insight into life; not an insipid moralist!"

"By these means we shall be doing what we can to enable a man, *if not to know any thing*, at least to make the most of what he does know!"

These extracts are not meant to imply that there is no truth in Mr. Lowe's remarks,—but only to show that the truth is so mixed up with what Plato would call "relative non-entity," in other words—crudity and error, as to effect little more than the investing these last with a dangerous plausibility.

INTRODUCTION.

A TRANSLATION of the following dialogue at the present moment may seem to need a few words of justification. It is obvious that at a time when the subject of education more than ever forces itself on public notice, its true nature and objects should as far as possible be agreed on and understood; and such understanding may be most easily arrived at by carefully distinguishing the genuine article from the spurious as tested by experience; in other words, by following the clear line of separation here traced between the philosopher and the Sophist, but which many eminent men of the present day are forward to cancel and forget. The word "Sophist" means generally educator or public teacher. Mr. Grote, in his History of Greece[1] gives a summary of the data from which its original significancy may be collected, showing its use in the general sense of a wise man, a clever man,—one

[1] Vol. viii. p. 479.

standing prominently before the public as an instructor, and in any form of discourse or composition communicating his wisdom to others. Nor did those who afterwards, in a more specific sense, bore this title differ much, at least to superficial observation, from the original type. "The men whom modern writers set down as 'the Sophists,' were not," says Mr. Grote, "distinguished in any marked or generic way from those so styled before them;[1] they only brought to the task a larger range of knowledge, and a more impressive power of speech and composition." The earlier and more conspicuous of their number were certainly some of the most eminent teachers of antiquity, objects of enthusiastic admiration to their contemporaries during the most brilliant age of Greece. They systematised the earlier instruction, making it more copious and accurate. Moreover, the general notions forming the basis of their teaching were an inevitable, and, in some respects, advantageous step in the history of philosophy, denoting that period when the human mind, instead of being absorbed in the contemplation of outward nature, or blindly following habit and tradition, turns round upon itself, and asserts its intrinsic dignity and supremacy.[2] But

[1] See Grote, History of Greece, vol. viii., p. 486.
[2] Now generally styled the rise of subjectivism,—the German "aufklärerei," or first stage of rationalism. In this, its earliest condition, it usually appears unaccompanied with faith, and chiefly

INTRODUCTION. 3

there are two ways of treating an intellectual discovery, which is apt on its first revelation to the consciousness to dazzle and mislead. The provisional emancipation of the soul from external trammels, whether natural or artificial, is undoubtedly a step in the right direction, but the eventual realisation of its rightful authority as free reason depends on the way in which this first step is followed up. One way of doing so is to make the acquisition of practical utilities and showy accomplishments the primary aim, in ignorance or distrust of any absolute test or rule of truth and right, and so carelessly adopting the standards of current opinion; another to look more especially to the improvement of the soul itself, striving to exalt its powers and purify its aspirations rather than adorn it with accomplishments, and in a sense reversing its newly gained notions of supremacy, by teaching it to look yet higher than itself, and to found its best claim to superiority on the consciousness of deficiency and want. Both of these processes may be popularly termed education; but one is comparatively limited, technical, and secular; the other is a less showy but

negative; it imports little more than the overthrow of preceding tradition and philosophy, and the utilitarian assertion of sceptical individualism; in Socrates and Plato it comes before us for the first time in a positive form as a new philosophy, or faith in ideal truth, based on the self conscious agency of soul; in its third stage, as superinduced by social discouragement among the Stoicks, Epicureans, etc., it threatened return to its first sceptical condition,—the mind's self-reliance in defiant opposition to the external.

more serious enterprise, initiating a new mental life, and offering—if men would only see it—a solution of the long pending difficulty about the connection of education with religion.

Sophistry is said by Plato to be hard to define, for false teaching assumes innumerable forms, and appears with very diversified characteristics. It consists in no particular doctrine, but rather in a general frame of mind, causing insincerity of thought and perversity of argument which induce a family likeness among many doctrinal differences and modes of teaching. The ancient Greek Sophist had peculiarities of his own corresponding to the circumstances of his time. In a playful vein of literally chopping or subdividing logic, he is described by Plato as one ostensibly wise and accomplished undertaking to make others wise, a hunter or fisher of men, a trader in arts and sciences, teaching argumentative skill or political knowledge in a disputatious or dialectical form, doing this for money, doing it systematically and professionally, and carrying these professional pretensions in huckstering fashion from city to city. All this, however, though certainly including the most obvious marks of the cotemporary Sophist, implied nothing essentially blameable, being indeed the necessary accompaniment of all teaching at the time; for instance, the negative Elenchus, or teaching by disputation and cross-examination, and so purifying the crude and confused intellect by accurately testing and winnowing its preconceptions, was common to the Sophists and to Socrates himself. So close, indeed, is the apparent resemblance between the Socratic and Sophistical forms of teaching, that Mr. Grote, after reading the Platonic dialogue on the subject, arrives at the deliberate conclusion that the definition there given "suits Socrates himself better than any other person known to us."[1] Yet this really touches only the outside of the subject. It was not any of these traits, or all of them together, which ultimately gave the Sophist a bad name, though certainly including those most open to superficial remark, all in fact that the vulgar eye was capable of appreciating. A more important issue was really at stake. It was the crisis between scepticism and idealism, between true education and false, between utilitarianism and true morality; for morality is indissolubly connected with the general aims of philosophy, and without belief in more than can be apprehended by the senses, its very bases, or the possible existence of obligation and of virtue, becomes as precarious and hopeless as that of a general truth. There was indeed a positive as well as a negative side in the Sophistical teaching as there was in the Socratic; but the former was only external indoctrination, the latter became the germ of a new phi-

[1] History, Vol. viii. p. 493. Also in his Plato, Vol. ii. p. 428.

losophy. Sophistry was condemned so as to become a bye-word to succeeding ages only when philosophy took a step beyond it, disowning from this truer and higher position its own rudimentary antecedents. Then only was the Sophist stigmatised as an impostor, parading a hypocritical imitation or caricature of philosophy, a mountebank affecting to sell what was really priceless, and putting forth a spurious article in full consciousness of its deficiency.

The intellectual condition of Athens in the age of the Sophists is the best key to the seeming ambiguity of their position, and this was intimately connected with its political state. In all progressive societies there comes a time when the ancient ties of tradition and sentiment,—the leading-strings of law and institution, no longer suffice to maintain their well-being; when personal pretension and ambition growing with increase of wealth, power, and knowledge, the nation may be said to be nearing its maturity through the comparatively riper consciousness of its individual members. So long as reason slumbers we assume the customary to be the right; only when a wider horizon opens do we suspect the possibility of error, and are led by comparison to discover, many of our notions and usages to be foolishness. At such a juncture, which is in fact the crisis of a new political birth, everything depends on what the individual essentially is; whether he be a mere political cypher or slave let loose with dangerously enlarged capacities of mischief, or whether his reason has been so cultivated as to supply from within that wholesome direction and stability which in earlier times was impressed or engrafted from without. The question is that of education, or rather, of true education and morality as opposed to spurious;—one leaving the individual selfish and self-satisfied with mere acquisitions of useful or showy accomplishment; the other making him intrinsically better, and more able to apprehend the reason and order representing the interests of all. This crisis few, if any, among the nations have hitherto successfully passed; the decay of old ties and associations usually leaving behind only broken links of the social chain, a number of irregular wills each claiming a greater relative share of power, in short, a chaos of mutually repellent or possibly hostile units, so that to escape the intolerable confusion engendered by a scramble for "rights" amidst the wild anarchy of capricious individualism, men readily close with the preferable alternative of forcible authority or tyranny. Such was notoriously the case among the states of ancient Greece as they successively advanced to wealth and power, the routine of aristocratic formalism became effete, yet without a corresponding growth of ability for self-government in the multitude; so that most of the cities fell into the hands of absolute rulers or "tyrants," and it was only under exceptional circumstances that in Athens the struggle was prolonged, leaving its historically recorded oscillations as a warning example for later ages. Here, in the age of Pericles, a virtual autocrat governing by persuasion, opportunity seemed to be afforded for a happier solution of the problem. The consciousness of superiority engendered by colonial wealth and maritime power was certainly here accompanied by a considerable amount of mental culture; poetry, architecture, and sculpture had attained unexampled excellence, so that Athens had become a vast museum, and an intense feeling for the beautiful was developed among its citizens. But these promising indications rested on a precarious foundation, threatening under ordinary circumstances to become the precursors of decline. The advance hitherto made had been accompanied by a perpetual decay of the ancient respect for institution and religion, poetry and art both contributing their share to relax the severity of traditional belief, which partly through their agency, in combination with other influences, underwent more or less arbitrary modifications. Even Homer had treated the gods with considerable licence; the growth of art was throughout a tacit conspiracy against the no longer understood forms of an uncouth symbolism, and the tendency of the later lyric and dramatic poetry more especially was to create a virtually new religion of moral sentiment within the nominal framework of the old.[1] But a merely artistic or sentimental education was quite insufficient to give permanency to the democratic edifice which Pericles had contributed to raise.[2] For art may act in two ways, either as a gratification for the selfish, or as an elementary sentimental education leading to higher developments of reason. The crisis was suspended while Pericles lived, and asserted the claims of reason and moderation by his personal influence. But the case altered when his place was occupied by political adventurers, who, like the obstreperous Cleon, or dissolute Alcibiades, found it easier to practise obsequious cajolery than to direct a rational administration. The successes of unscrupulous ambition which promoted the extension of Athenian empire subverted the general respect for law and right, until public selfishness degenerated into private, and political profligacy descended to the level of individuals.[3] The demoralisation

[1] See Zeller's Hist. Greek Philosophy, 2nd ed., vol. ii. p. 6, 9, etc.
[2] "Where an unclean mind carries virtuous qualities," says Shakspeare, "there commendations go with pity; they are virtues and traitors too."
[3] Mr. Grote's abrupt denial of Athenian demoralisation seems paradoxical; indeed, at p. 539 note of the eighth vol. of his History he quotes Plato, Repub. 6,492 *sq.* in proof of the contrary. Although much good feeling was exhibited at the restoration under Thrasybulus, still the patriotic efforts of the time were like the struggles of a

sometimes ascribed to the plague which broke out among the overcrowded population during the first years of the Peloponnesian war, but which in truth was rather revealed than caused by that calamity,[1] henceforth went on unchecked, affording the best opportunity and encouragement for sophistical teaching.

Ordinary Athenian education had hitherto consisted of two branches, entitled respectively gymnastics and music; the latter including all the then known culture of the muse, such as readings and recitations from the poets, with the moral instruction thence generally derivable; but there was no ready access to higher attainments; and morals and politics in particular were for the most part left to the casual teaching of family precept and social example.[2] But the more wide-spread the average culture, and the greater the prizes to be won by ambition, the more necessary it became for ambitious ability to seek exceptional means of distinction; and this want the race of professional teachers or Sophists undertook to

drowning man, and the death of Socrates blurs the picture; not progressive reform, but conservative revival and pragmatical legalism were the remedies appealed to.

[1] Thucydides (2, 53) significantly describes the men of the day as unable, under the trial of pestilence, to persevere or hold out in allegiance to the fine or becoming (τὸ καλὸν), because no one knew whether he should not perish before he;h ad reached it; *i.e.* the man was not morally won; the end, the fin shed form of excellence, was something external; the essential principle, which alone is lasting and reliable, was wanting.

[2] Plato, Protagoras, ch. 42, 43; Sophistes, p. 230.

supply. They offered to their pupils a far more extended range of acquirements than had hitherto been accessible, together with unusual facilities for obtaining skill in argument and public speaking; in short, the knowledge and ability especially needed by the man of the world and politician. But this was far from being all that was really wanted. Occurring at the time of general displacement and transition above alluded to, when old opinions were obsolete and new ones unformed, it only increased the prevailing unsettlement,[1] making the lack of fixed principle more painfully conspicuous. The self-consciously clever and accomplished man could no longer be expected to submit to the legislative caprices of the many, or to accept with unquestioning deference the traditions of antiquity. Erudition and the art of rhetoric afforded weapons to unscrupulous pugnacity, but no basis whatever of social cohesion; for this a higher sort of education was needed, such as at the time in question was neither sought for nor understood. The will fluctuated at random with no safe anchorage. The previous philosophy, both Dorian and Ionian, had laid the foundations of scepticism in the common discovery of the inability of

[1] The philosopher as well as the Sophist was suspected and hated by the steady-going citizen. Mr. Mill, Essays, vol. iii. p. 311, has some good remarks on this feeling, which instinctively disapproved all teaching except that certified by some recognised authority as safe and orthodox. The reasons of the philosopher for disliking ordinary teachers or Sophists were of a different and indeed opposite character.

the senses to grasp abiding truth; the phenomenal world was aptly compared to the flow of a stream perpetually shifting, and so defying admeasurement and comprehension; while the changeless "One" suggested by reason to Xenophanes and Parmenides seemed a vain paradox, which the ingenuity of Zeno could only support by shewing the greater logical extravagances attaching to the contrary opinion. But his arguments availed little so long as the title-deeds of a higher philosophy were wanting in the uncertainty which prevailed as to the specific agency and objects of reason; there needed some sort of positive evidence for the existence and reliability of the higher faculty now beginning to be recognised for the first time. And, perhaps, the speculative theories of the Sophists, negative and unsatisfactory as they were, may be accounted a first step in this direction. For as Anaxagoras had vaguely recognised the existence of mind in nature, so by them man's general ability was asserted, though without any firm belief or examination into the nature of the assumed standard. Somewhat as Berkeley from the sensational premises of Locke inferred the unreality of the external, so Protagoras from the premises of Heraclitus as to the changing character of sensible phenomena deduced the universal subjectivity of knowledge; the movements and external appearances of things comprising all we apprehend or are entitled to say about them, and these varying with the circumstances and condition of the observer, it follows that "man is sole measure of all things," of all that is, and also all that is not; in other words, there can be no objective truth, nor any real falsehood. Gorgias is said to have arrived at similar inferences from the data of Parmenides, and indeed to have written a treatise on non-entity, in which he endeavoured to prove the unreality and impossibility of existence as well as of non-existence from the logical difficulties inherent in the respective conceptions. For, in the first place, it seems contradictory and absurd to say the non-existent *is* or exists; secondly, the existent must needs be either one or many, begun or without beginning; if without beginning it must be infinite, consequently uncontained either by another or by itself, and so nowhere or virtually non-existent; begun it cannot be, for nothing can come of nothing; nor can it even come from the existing, for then "the existing" would be subject to alteration and change, and so in effect be non-existent. The predicates of unity and plurality were similarly disposed of; and from the apparently undeniable position that one cannot be also many, it was inferred that no communion can exist among ideas, or that all predication is impossible,[1] Euthydemus is said to have

[1] See Sophistes, p. 251ᵇ; Zeller's Gr. Phil. vol. i. p. 764. It must be recollected that even in Plato's time the relation of names and conceptions to things, and particularly the ambiguity of the copula, *is*,—were

maintained on similar grounds the contrary proposition, namely, that all predicates are always alike true, so that there can be no real distinction between false and true, good and evil;[1] for the great Parmenides had laid it down that non-entity must not be said *to be;* it is unknowable, unthinkable, unpronounceable; he who asserts anything says necessarily something *is*, and he who says what is says the truth; consequently it is impossible to think or say what *is not*, or, in other words, what is false and self-contradictory.

It should be remembered that Plato's portrait of the Sophist imports a general type of character—not a literal representation of individuals; and although Mr. Grote may be right in saying that there was no homogeneous party or tangible school leagued together under the standard of "Die Sophistik" to teach immorality and untruthfulness, it is no less certain that then, as now, the tendency of a merely ornamental culture, grafted on a root of scepticism, was liable to mislead, and that the axiom attributed to Protagoras was alone sufficient to engender among less conscientious teachers, the futilities and turpitudes ordinarily attaching to the Sophistical

far from being understood. Mediæval nominalism betokened a great revolution in philosophy as well as theology—becoming the starting point of new developments of realistic philosophy as well as of experimental science, the proved unreliability of names enforcing greater attention to things.

[1] Plato, Cratylus, 386ᵈ.

character. Scepticism has an infectious charm for superficial minds, and they who have themselves come to despair of truth, are constantly tempted to try to reduce others to the same hopeless condition; this they endeavour to do, either indirectly, as by claiming a monopoly of attention for practical matters and "useful information," or else directly, by overwhelming inexperienced reasoners by artful confutation. For this they ply the elementary mechanism of discourse, rejoicing in intricacies of grammar and logic, of words and syllogisms, as an exercise of their dexterity; and hence the Eristic art, which became so generally popular in Greece about this period, and which was indeed only a more comprehensive name for the Sophistic, as including idle amateurs, while the other title denoted professional remuneration.[1] The later Sophists abandoned the educational earnestness of the older, using their sceptical results for rhetorical purposes to meet the requirements of fraud or frivolity; and hence the more repulsive forms of disputatious cavilling met with in Plato's Euthydemus and Aristotle's sophistical "Elenchi." It seemed at last to be the great object of the cotemporary teacher to confuse and baffle opponents, and to make everything doubtful and uncertain.[2] But though the same form of

[1] See Sophistes, pp. 225ᵈ, 235ᶜ, 232ᵇ.
[2] περὶ πάντων ὅλως ἀμφισβητεῖν." See Sophist. pp. 225ᶜ, 230, 231ᵃ, 232ᵇ. Repub. 5 p. 454ᵃ.

disputation was common to the caviller (Eristicus) and the philosopher, the resemblance was only apparent,—sophistical discussion bearing much the same resemblance to philosophical as the wolf to the hound,[1] or as one who wantonly destroys to one winning sustenance for his master. The object of the former was pursued irrespectively of truth and fairness, confounding an adversary by logical quibbles learned by heart for the purpose; the equivocal meaning of words supplying inexhaustible resources to the unscrupulous disputant, while it was always easy to shift or to disguise the real issue. He would confound subject and predicate, or, as instanced in the main quibble of the following dialogue, elicit a predicate out of the copula distinct from the real predicate;[2] he would press for facts in preference to metaphysical fancies, or insist on the necessity of following strictly the inferences of reason, and adhering to the rules of logic even in spite of the testimony of the senses.[3] It were vain to recapitulate here the varieties of subterfuge of which an artful pleader may avail himself, and of which Aristotle's Rhetoric affords a rich collection. He

[1] Sophist. 231ᵃ. Comp. Repub. 5, 454ᵃ.
[2] See Sophistes, p. 240.
[3] See examples in Mill's Logic, vol. i., 2nd Edition, p. 104, of ambiguities which, though now suggesting no difficulty, seemed very perplexing to persons encountering them for the first time. The appeal to fact against reason is the characteristic challenge of the modern Sophist, a consequence of the materialistic tendencies of present opinion.

may assert the argument to be irrelevant, or that he knew it before, and knew it as confuted ; he may astutely shift the issue, as Dr. Mill in an elaborate work once affected to confute the Biblical criticism of Strauss, by denouncing it as an advocacy of Pantheism ; he may try to damage his opponent's credit by harping on some flaw or exaggeration in a collateral or unimportant part of his argument, or else substitute raillery for argument, as by contemptuous allusions to Thucydides, or the absurdity of teaching theology by arithmetic. "'Tis ridiculous," says Bacon, "to see what shifts these formalists have, what prospectives to make superficies to seem body that hath depth and bulk." Each age and turn of circumstance has its own peculiarly adapted forms of fallacy or false semblance, aptly called by Plato the hiding away in abysses of fantastic unreality and non-entity, against which there is no conceivable safeguard save an adequate acquaintance with reality and entity,— in other words, such a philosophical education of opinion as may convict mendacity on the instant, and put pretentious charlatanism to the blush.

To the sophistical cavil of the dialogue, where scepticism appears in the converse of its usual form, asserting, not that "nothing is," but that non-entity is not, and that consequently falsehood is impossible,

Plato replies that non-entity does exist, and that very unmistakeably and mischievously in a certain way,[1] namely, as the "other" of the true, a spirit especially affecting the garb of language and discourse, and in that investiture playing off its elvish pranks with exuberant vivacity; that its forms indeed are infinite, extending through all the "ideas," or, as we should say, categories or varieties of being, truth being in each instance identical and one, whereas to possible deviations from it there can be no limit. His argument implies an entirely different theory of being and of truth, namely, that of Socrates, which though essentially subjective, and agreeing in the current axiom of "man the measure," assumed man's capacity of measurement as able to realise far more than precarious estimates of opinion; treating it as a divine voice or faculty susceptible of becoming, through cultivation, a progressive revelation; so that Socrates may be said to have made the discovery of the soul, as distinguished from the mere blind assumption or barren recognition of it, inasmuch as its unseen essence becomes known only

---

[1] The phenomenal world is justly said "to be," but then its phenomena are of a qualified or relative nature, as music by night seems different from music by day, and as Touchstone says, what is a good life in one view is a very vile one in another. Cæsar, second in Rome, was in his own opinion nothing, yet in reality he was Cæsar still; and so Burges' translation of Plato may be said, in a certain sense, "to be," nay, perhaps, to exist as a translation; yet not, strictly speaking, as a translation of Plato; it is rather the "other" of Plato, yet at all events "existing" as Burges' view of Plato, and as printed paper.

INTRODUCTION. 19

through its operations and effects, and these operations were by him traced and systematised for the first time. The appearance of Socrates is said to have been altogether original and unique,[1] incomprehensible indeed to the sensuously fastidious Greek, from its incongruous combination of an ungainly exterior, compared by Alcibiades to that of a Silenus, with an inward beauty and majesty representing the ever aspiring soul of humanity itself; the one uncouth, prosaic, and pedantic; the other, harmonious, poetical, divine. Socrates was certainly no "sophist" in the common acceptation of the term; he pretended neither to know nor to teach; he professed only the art of spiritual midwifery, helping other men's souls to bring forth what was virtually in them, carefully separating the ore from the dross—the genuine progeny from the spurious brood of falsehood, and following out the Delphian axiom—"know thyself"—by weeding out erroneous conceptions, testing the accuracy of ideas by induction, and gathering up the net result in accurate generalisations or definitions. In short, the theory of true education, as distinguished from mere instruction or adventitious embellishment, was here broached for the first time; and the practice of dialectical discussion used for the

---

[1] The true teacher of virtue is described in the Meno, p. 100, as resembling Tiresias in the Shades, of whom Homer says—
  Οἷος πέπνυται—τοὶ δὲ σκιαὶ ἀΐσσουσι—
He alone has a soul to know—The rest are but flitting shades.

purpose had obviously quite a different meaning from that of the disputation of the Sophists, being a bracing exercise of the reasoning faculty, a process calculated to refresh and enlighten, rather then to weary and confound; a necessarily preliminary to a reliable philosophy, one not to be abruptly closed by dogmatical inference and assertion, as if the aim were attained and the subject finished, but to be unremittingly pursued in the confident spirit of ideal love continually seeking a higher truth beyond.[1] It was this noble confidence which led Plato—though persevering for the most part in the educational or dialectical method of his master—to think he had discovered, at least in an ideal outline, that essence of truth of which Socrates was incessantly in search; assuming the object of knowledge to be identical in nature with its instrument, and filling up the assumed outline by more or less superficial generalisation. For this he has been stigmatised as a dreamer, and certainly by an overhasty manipulation of ideal theory he may have produced what is in some respects a caricature, and have so supplied a basis for future dogmatisms; yet though thereby incurring much ignorant animadversion, there is an essential truth in his speculations making him the legitimate

[1] M. Bartholomès, in his work on Huet, enumerates three sorts of scepticism which it may be useful to remember:—1. Absolute scepticism or Pyrrhonism; 2. Theological or dogmatical scepticism, such as that of Bayle and nominalistic theology in general; 3. Philosophical scepticism.

INTRODUCTION. 21

fountain-head of true philosophy,[1] and in particular enabling him so to form a link of connection between the general and the special, as in some measure to bridge the gulf which the all abstract idealism of Parmenides had left open. To the immoveable, unimaginable "one" of the later he assigned plurality and movement, thereby bringing it conceptionally nearer to the actual; while at the same time insisting on an essential unity in plurality, through which alone science or knowledge becomes possible. For the fluctuating imagery alone exhibited to the senses cannot itself be the object of knowledge, since if it were, knowledge too would fluctuate, and in fact cease to be knowledge. The object of knowledge must be constant, something on which the mind can stand or rest, ($\dot{\epsilon}\pi\iota\sigma\tau\dot{\eta}\mu\eta$) in other words an ideal reality distinct from phenomena, yet forming their unseen pattern or basis. Yet in the midst of Plato's abstract ontological idealism there occur anticipatory glimpses of the dynamical idealism of Aristotle and the new Platonists;[2] an hypothesis now more than ever forced upon men of science by the progress of discovery, and one

[1] He stated the problem correctly, though erring in the filling up, of which so much still remains to be accomplished. But—"Auf die geistige Bestimmung des Ganzen wird die Untersuchung des einzelnen hinführen." See Trendelenburg, Logische Untersuchungen; also Von Baer, Reden, Vol. 1, pp. 272, 275; Oersted's Spirit of Nature (by Horner) p. 24.
[2] Sophist. 247e. Comp. Theæt. 184d; Cratylus, 387; Phædo, 105.

which cannot be dispensed with if spiritual things be contemplated at all. A greater familiarity with the results of mental agency thus tended to reconcile in a higher sphere the Eleatic with the Ionian or Heraclitean view of things, rendering the fusion of empirical opposites conceptionally possible. Were the real and true as entirely unconnected and contrasted with the false and phenomenal as Parmenides supposed, it certainly could not be said of the latter that "they are," and sophistry would get its required paradoxical justification out of the depths of metaphysics; if on the other hand being be really differentiated, as forming a true substratum to the phenomena resting on and partaking of it, then falsehood may also be said truly to exist as the "other" of the true, and neither in things nor in discourses can we expect to meet with absolute being or with pure truth,—nor again with absolute non-entity or unmixed falsehood; the two being associated together in endless varieties of proportion, so that it remains for the philosopher to restore as far as possible the sullied image of the true in its motley phenomenal manifestations[1] by ruthlessly exposing the abortive creations of thought and discourse affording lurking places for fallacy.

Instead, then, of denying the existence of any

[1] All colours, says Bacon, agree in the dark; but truth and falsehood resemble the iron and clay in the toes of Nebuchadnezzar's image; they may cleave, but they will not incorporate.

INTRODUCTION. 23

distinction between the Socratic school and the
Sophists whom it attacked, or at least any save one
appearing to the disadvantage of the former, we may
recognize between them the all important difference
separating true education and philosophy from the
narrowness of mere indoctrination or positivism, that
medley of speculative insipidity and presumption of
which the subjectivism and superficial rationalism
of modern England, Germany, and France has
afforded many instances. But a mind which is
itself essentially sceptical is naturally unable to see
the matter in its true light, or to recognise the *bonâ
fide* existence of a "fiend"—whether German or
Greek—reflecting what are substantially its own
conclusions. "The conclusions of Protagoras," says
Mr. Grote,[1] "were not improperly sceptical, but
perfectly just, ratified by the gradual abandonment
of ultra-phenomenal researches by the major part
of philosophers." On the contrary, it may be said
that the ablest philosophers,—even of physical in-
vestigators,—from Aristotle to Bacon and Claude
Bernard, disclaim the superficial denunciation of
metaphysics, nay, treat the phenomenal as chiefly
interesting from the indications afforded by it of a
subjacent reality; moreover, that no step even in
physical discovery can be made without the aid of
ideas and assumptions borrowed from this much

[1] History, vol. viii. p. 504.

abused department. Materialists and Positivists talk metaphysics without knowing it, their metaphysics being only the more presumptuous and frivolously incorrect from this very circumstance. They discourse freely of nature, matter, cause, law, force, space, and time, in innocent unconsciousness of the metaphysical nature of what they assume as the foundation of their reasonings; in other respects too sharing with infantine philosophy the mistake of confounding the perceptions of the senses with realities, and in reckless impatience abruptly closing the door which the more cautious enquirer would leave open. Little is the Positivist aware that while denouncing metaphysics he secretly cherishes a metaphysic of his own, but one of the coarsest and most trivial kind. He builds confidently on "facts," in assured conviction of knowing the external, forgetting the complicated telegraphic machinery intervening between the external object and his consciousness, and the difficulties inseparable from a sure interpretation of the signals. M. Berthelot[1] remarks that science does not exclude idealism, and that though no confusion should be permitted between heterogeneous departments, there may be an ideal science beyond the limits of the chain-work of empirical co-efficients where true causes and teleogical purpose may fairly have a claim to be

[1] See Revue de Deux Mondes, 15th November, 1863.

INTRODUCTION. 25

considered. Science needs materials; but it is the mind which builds up those materials into available forms, so as to constitute the science or knowledge vaunted by the Positivist or Sophist, but which, as educationally administered by him, are only an illusion,—the accumulation in a dead hand of the scientific capital which only active intellectual investment and circulation can render profitable or prolific.

It is vain to feed indolently on fruits dropped from the tree of knowledge, while at the same time borrowing nothing from the tree of life. Man's mental education consists essentially in hypothesis tested by observation. We set before us an ideal, and try to reach up to it;—imagine a prerogative instance and proceed to its verification. The discovery is, in truth, the prerogative of genius, or the correct exercise of the ideal faculty,—the power of a soul inspired by the Platonic Eros to create an intellectual world within itself. Hence it has been truly said that religion and poetry were man's earliest teachers, since they are the expression of his earliest ideals. Nor is it to the rudiments of civilization that the function of imagination is confined; it accompanies each stage in its career, and philosophy itself is so far indebted to it as to admit of being called the poetry of reason,[1] a discovery of true representations

[1] Poetry, says Bacon, is history written by the imagination; true history is the basis of philosophy. De Augm., 2, 13; and Descriptio Globi Intellectualis, chap. 3.

or images, whereas those of ordinary poetry are, to a great extent, fantastic and fallacious. The mental movement resembles the bodily. As in walking we advance a foot and draw after it the other, so in science, an idea or hypothesis is advanced, which, if bearing the test of subsequent verification, carries the whole mind along with it. All human progress depends on this initial capacity of movement, or of self-elevation beyond the immediately known and present to something unknown and distant; a power which, though continually compelled to retrace its steps in order to establish and secure its footing, never rests satisfied with the dead materials or results alone contemplated in sophistical education, but pauses only for the moment in order to test the accuracy of the intellectual tie supplied out of the resources of thought, and on whose correspondence with the true nature and demarcations of things, as opposed to mere arbitrary divisions of them, Plato was the first to insist.[1] The aim of philosophy, says Trendelenburg,[2] is to survey the particular from the vantage ground of the general, tacitly assuming this general to be a thought analogous to its own, extending through and overruling all phenomenal parts. Empirical science, on the other hand, scrutinises the parts, assuming in turn that each of

---

[1] Comp. *e.g.*, Plato's Politicus, p, 262, 263, with Bacon's De Augm., 3, chap. iv.
[2] Logische Untersuchungen.

INTRODUCTION. 27

these has certain individual peculiarities requiring cautious premeditation. As knowledge progresses this divergency of view tends to disappear, the investigation of particulars being, in fact, the only real way to the full elucidation of the general; the latter is not to be understood at once, it can only be provisionally stated as a problem; and man's limited powers being immediately adapted to deal only with limited subjects, it is only through special scientific investigations that knowledge is safely increased. But this is not exactly the course taken by human ingenuity; its first efforts are, on the contrary, directed to a comprehension of the general—indeed, the largest generality—and since this comprehension is, strictly speaking, for the moment impossible, a number of more or less vague and unsubstantial hypotheses or systems result, each surveying the problem from a peculiar and more or less limited point of view, and so inevitably illusory and contradictory, explaining some phenomena but not others, and by their inconsistencies and failures discrediting for a time the very name of philosophy itself. Experimental verification occupies so large and so prominent a space in the construction of science, that we are apt to disparage or forget the initial power on which all depends; so that at last it seems as if the legitimate aim of the "Elenchus" were not only to correct, but to supersede the ideal faculty itself.[1] Yet every enterprise of discovery must be preceded by a mental conception or speculative plan, calculated, as far as may be, to comprehend the particular observations, and to unite them in an intelligible whole. And so far as the proposed conception corresponds with observed phenomena, and is really adequate to its purpose, it will itself be found to lead the way to some wider generalisation, just as the limb or bone, really and properly understood by an Owen or a Cuvier, tells the tale of the organized form to which it belonged. And thus the illusory lights of premature inconsistent systems may be expected to disappear, but only to merge in the more enduring radiance of a wider truth, as the range of outstanding possibilities becomes reduced by observation to narrower limits, and the infinite series of the phenomenal is approximately exhausted.

The most serious objection made to the sophistical teaching is its immoral tendency. This charge Mr. Grote denies, because not recognising any essential difference between moral philosophy, or morals founded on principle, and popular morality, or the morality of custom, sentiment, and precept; the latter a very imperfect discipline under any circumstances, and tending through the initial misconception as to the nature of the object to degenerate

[1] Compare Mr. Mill's language—Essays, vol. iii. pp. 336, 337.

more and more till it either resigns the field to chance or plods onwards in the direction of casuistry; that art of paltering with conscience, instructing it how far it may safely go, that is, not how good, but how bad we may venture to be, and now cheat the devil while enjoying ourselves to the utmost.[1] It is this view looking at morality as consisting in outward act rather than in the intention and the will, which has not only produced church corruption, but misled even impartial Theorists, making them suppose it to be something relative and fluctuating with times and circumstances, instead of being inalterable and immutable. True morality is in the soul or in the unalterable principle, not in physiology or social economy, or other varieties of relations and practical applications; and this was the true meaning of Socrates in identifying morality and science, meaning by the word not empirical science, but ideal truth or certainty. "What, after all," asks Mr. Grote, "was the real teaching of this much-abused class of men? Who has not read the Choice of Hercules by Prodicus, that well-known fable found in every book professing to collect impressive lessons of elementary morality?" Then look at the Platonic dialogue on

---

[1] Hence it was said of the Jesuitical moralist who had succeeded in making a difficult task an easy one:—
　　　　Veut-on monter aux célestes tours?
　　　　Chemin pierreux est grande rêverie;
　　　　Escobar nous le fait de velours.

Protagoras; "this alone suffices to shew that Plato did not conceive the Sophist to be an unworthy or incompetent teacher,—since he represents him as professing to teach 'good counsel' in domestic and family relations, and how to speak and act in the most effective way for the welfare of the city." "As soon as the child understands what is said to it," says Protagoras in the Dialogue,[1] "the nurse, mother, or tutor, tries in every way to make it good, taking occasion from every occurrence and word, and pointing out—this is right, this is wrong, this is honourable, this dishonourable; do this, do not do that. And if they obey what is said, it is well; if not, they set them right with threats and blows;" a process afterwards repeated by the laws on a larger scale. But this is legality, not morality;[2] a discipline enforcing the precarious service of a slave or mercenary condottiere in the train of virtue, not the free allegiance of a patriot voluntarily enlisted in her cause; it is but the temporary bent of an elastic rod, readily and inevitably recoiling on loosening the string—

"He who abstains from bad actions from fear of punishment,
Will assuredly commit the same if he get an opportunity"—

said the Stoic Cleanthes;[3] and so far and no farther

[1] Protag. 325, 326.
[2] Compare what Plato says of the coarse manipulations of legality (Politicus, p. 295) with Kant's Critique of Practical Vernunft, i. 1, 2. Mr. Grote speaks (Hist. 8, 509) of psephisms, indictments, and dikasteries, as forming a constituent element of the "morality" of Athens!
[3] See Stobœus Serm., 6, 19.

extended the sophistical teaching of morals; belief and principle were wanting; the motive was not placed within, but had to be supplied by force or self-interest from without. Mr. Grote entirely misconceives the matter when fancying it a sufficient justification of the Sophists to say that the doctrine attributed to Callicles in the Gorgias, openly defending the right of the strongest, was not advocated by them, and could not have been so advocated in defiance of law and institution by any public speaker at Athens; since the condition of legality, in which violence is only restrained by fear, supposes an already corrupt condition of the popular mind, and the state of legal security considered by materialists as moral, is only the same principle of force applied in another form. There is no alternative but that of either rising with Socrates, or sinking through successive stages of decline, in company with Polus, Thrasymachus, and Callicles. It seems strange to find Mr. Mill,[1] himself a writer on Ethics, endorsing the notion that a generally lax state of morality justifies a professional teacher in teaching accordingly; as if it were not rather his bounden duty to lead on to juster views,

[1] Essays, vol. iii. 305, 306, 307, etc. Mr. Mill here insinuates that a higher morality is nothing but cant, and that the Sophists were justified in repeating that successful injustice is no evil. He approves (p. 224) Mr. Grote's saying that Plato's testimony against the Sophists, even were it stronger than it is, has no value against them, unless we extend our condemnation to the ways of mankind in general;" but this is just what the true moral teacher—aiming at reality, not mere seeming—necessarily does.

instead of merely propagating the false sentiment immediately surrounding him. Mr. Grote admits that the Platonic Protagoras appears, from the sequel of the dialogue of that name, to be unacquainted with Ethical theory, and to that extent to be disqualified from teaching it; but this makes all the difference, inasmuch as the knowing the reason of a thing differs from knowing it merely as a rule or routine; the latter is mechanical and servile, the former free, reliable, and organic. Morals, as vulgarly meant, may undoubtedly be inculcated in a preliminary way, and, to a certain extent, in descriptions of duties or virtues,—as expounded in school Philosophies, or in elementary works of biography and history, or exemplified from the drama, or practically communicated in family or national association. Gorgias is accordingly said to have set the example in antiquity of casuistical enumeration and definition of the virtues, and Hippias to have written a treatise on the same subject in the form of a dialogue between Nestor and Neoptolemus.[1] But morality cannot really be taught in this loose admonitory way; it is a matter of conviction; its material contents are no doubt an external

---

[1] The morality so taught, says Mr. Grote (p. 521), might be too high, perhaps, but certainly would not err on the side of corruption. Polus, too, was morally right, *for he defended the common tastes and sentiments of every man in Greece! Again common opinion!—the fundamental principle of sawgrinder's ethics.*

INTRODUCTION. 33

erudition more or less correctly generalized from ordinary or scientific experience, as Socrates himself referred to custom, law, and utility, to fill up the moral outline; but all these are relative and variable, like the relative tallness and smallness of Simmias and Socrates; and if it be no more than this—if it be not firmly rooted in the character and reason—it is but the phantom of what it pretends to be.[1] Mr. Grote does glance at a certain fundamental difference of view between Plato and the Sophists, but only to the disparagement of the former in comparison with the solid and serviceable instruction conveyed by the others. "Plato's peculiar views," he says, "brought him into inevitable collision not only with the Sophists but with all the leading agents by whom the business of life was carried on." Very naturally, for his object was to make men good, theirs only to form practical politicians or good men of business. "They taught men to think, speak, and act in *Athens*,—of course accepting as the basis of their teaching that type of character which estimable men exhibited and the public approved in Athens; not

[1] Plato well describes it in the Republic (vii. p. 518) as a wheeling round of the whole man from the perishable to the light of the real, or to the form of good. Mr. Mill agrees with Mr. Grote in espousing the doctrine of Protagoras as to virtue being something universally and spontaneously taught by all men to all men,—in short, to be picked up at random in the common intercourse of life (Essays, vol. iii. p. 297), or through the omnipotent agency of king Nomos. Socrates, adds Mr. Mill, considering justice, virtue, etc., as *things whose meaning still remains to be found out*, of course contests the point with Protagoras, but only, he thinks, in a utilitarian sense.

undertaking to recast the type, but to arm it with new capacities and adorn it with fresh accomplishments." But this is the very essence of the charge against the Sophists, that at a time when the minds of men had out-grown the limits of the ancient discipline, and all depended on individual attainment of a capacity of moral self-government, these teachers continued to work assiduously in the old groove, attempting only to better and enlarge the scale of outward proficiency; that in the midst of the intellectual revolution which they assuredly contributed to promote, they assumed in some respects a reactionary and generally an acquiescent attitude; teaching virtue after the customary antiquated fashion, of which their own professional status proclaimed the insufficiency. For had custom, tradition, and association been sufficient for the purpose, no extraordinary teachers would have been needed. "Exhortation," says Mr. Grote[1] himself, "is useless with dull minds ignorant of their own ignorance; so long as a man believes himself to be wise, you may lecture for ever without making an impression on him; you must first change the attitude of his mind by making him feel his ignorance on subjects which he fancies he knows; and this is best effected by the negative Elenchus, suitably preparing the way for positive teaching."[2] What

[1] Plato, vol. ii. p. 409. [2] Comp. Sophist, p. 230.

availed it to instil old traditional lessons of sobriety and probity, or to repeat by rote the well-remembered axioms of Hesiod or Simonides, when men had lost their customary habits of belief, and were looking for some new foundation on which morality might be based; not a mere set of wise saws and precepts, such as children repeat by rote from primer and copy book, and which may now be met with in the sub-departments of casuistical theology, but something appealing to conviction, and so calculated to become an integral element of the soul adopting it; in short, not a drilled lesson, but a living abiding principle. It may be thought that utilitarianism offers such a principle; yet this, however explained or refined, is in itself no *moral* principle at all; it is but a more or less adroit selfishness guided in its choice by considerations of physical fitness. The bases of morality are wanting; there is no free initiative or soul, no adequate authority or law; for the moral law is necessarily absolute, and within the sphere of phenomenal relativities no absolute rule is to be found. We are here compelled to have resource to an ideal world considered as underlying the phenomenal; an hypothesis which, while admitting every thing in the latter to be rigorously determined by its physical antecedents, allows the possibility of free and final causation, or true moral initiation and regulation, in the unknown conditions of the former.

Such an hypothesis occupies a just mean between supernaturalism and utilitarianism, possessing the rationality absent from the one, and the elevation in which the other is deficient. Morality is thus effectually based upon religion; for the essence of religion is idealism, belief in the unseen, in the existence of a soul and of a moral order quite independently of sectarian controversies and dogmatical definitions. Nor are the claims of utilitarianism denied, they are only subordinated; precedence is given to an ideal principle; but the principle is a mine for intelligence to work, an unseen rule which must be subjectively expounded and appropriated; either in the form of moral maxims having various degrees of universality and applicability, or in those generalisations of physical science which must ever be invoked as affording in a ministerial capacity the only available criterion for the solution of practical problems.

Mr. Grote professes inability to see any essential distinction between the philosopher and sophist except in the circumstance that the latter taught for pay, thereby incurring the enmity of unpaid rivals, and increasing the odium already attaching to the name from other causes. He begins his elaborate vindication of the ill-used class by the remark,[1] that

---

[1] History, vol. viii. pp. 475-482. Also Plato, vol. ii. p. 430. Mr. Mill too says (Essays, 3, p. 314) that Plato's antipathy to

among those engaged in different lines of intellectual labour,—the speculative and the practical men of Athens,—there subsisted a standing controversy and spirit of detraction, and that even between different teachers in the same intellectual walk there often prevailed acrimonious feelings. He proceeds to describe how the originally innocent or rather laudatory significancy of the word sophist was afterwards obscured by the jealousy of new ideas and superior knowledge characteristic of an ignorant democracy,—a feeling countenanced and encouraged by the genius of Aristophanes, by whom these meritorious teachers were indiscriminately assailed. The result was that along with its originally comprehensive sense there grew up in connection with it a certain invidious feeling, a circumstance not sufficiently attended to by modern authors, who, blindly led by the insinuations of Aristophanes, make no allowance for that force of literary and philosophical antipathy which at Athens was no less real and constant than the political."

"Now the Sophists," continues Grote, "incurred a double measure of this antipathy by receiving pay; a fact provocative of envy, to some extent, even

the Sophists was founded on this circumstance alone, but afterwards admits the existence of another cause, namely, their dealing with apparent, not real knowledge; he however retorts the imputation of unreality, treating Plato's conception of knowledge as visionary and useless, opposed not to Sophistry, either in the ancient or modern acceptation of the term, but only to common-place.

among those deriving nothing from them, but still more among inferior members of their own profession. Even Socrates and Plato, though much superior to any such envy, cherished a genuine and vehement aversion to receiving pay for teaching," which they considered a degradation, depriving the office of all its freedom and its charm. "They therefore considered the name Sophist so denoting intellectual celebrity, combined with an odious association, as one pre-eminently suited to the leading teachers for pay. They *stole* the name out of general circulation in order to fasten it, along with other discreditable attributes, upon their opponents, the paid teachers; although it is certain that if, in the middle of the Peloponnesian war, an Athenian had been asked, who are the principal Sophists in your city? he would have named Socrates among the first."

It would seem from this that Mr. Grote does consider the Platonic condemnation of the Sophist as having proceeded, after all, in no slight degree from motives of professional jealousy, availing itself of vulgar prejudice in order to cast unmerited discredit on paid opponents. "If," argues Mr. Grote, "the receiving pay be held to be a reproach, it will assuredly bear hard upon the great body of modern teachers, who are led to embrace their profession and to discharge its important duties — like other professional men — by the prospect of either deriving an income from it, or of making a figure in it, or both." Dr. Whewell[1] declares that he sees nothing coarse or degrading in receiving payment for education any more than in the paid services of a forensic advocate or minister of religion; Professor Zeller, too, observes that the Greeks themselves paid their poets, painters, and musicians; and that even the Olympic victor was not ashamed to collect subscriptions. He adds that the educator is degraded by receiving compensation, only when immediately dependent on individual pupils, who are likely enough to make a short-sighted or selfish estimate of the values of different studies; whereas, in case of public officials receiving government salaries the circumstances are altered. Yet he well knows how a distinguished living professor of his own university was prosecuted for a valuable historical publication, and how Spinoza declined a chair in the same university on this very ground—that it was essentially impossible to obey two masters, namely, reason and conventionalism, at the same time, or to reconcile the duties of a faithful investigator of truth with those of a sound Churchman. Mr. Grote does not even ask whether Plato had any reason for his scrupulosity, although he must be aware that it was from absence of such

[1] Plato, vol. ii. p. 7.

delicacy, and by putting instruction on the low footing of official teaching that most of the corruptions of educational establishments have arisen. If, indeed, the desired education be viewed in the light of a commercial transaction, or as mere accomplishments to be conferred or given, there may be a fair pretext for insisting on a remunerative *quid pro quo*, although even in this case the issue depending on a confidential trust beyond the reach of money, there is always a risk of deterioration of the quality of the teaching in deference to the prejudices of the taught.[1] But if education be not so much a communication of results or varnish of accomplishment, as the kindling the spirit of a new life or love of truth in congenial minds,[2]—this, which is really above all price, and which can only be effected by one similarly minded and loving truth for its own sake, ought in strictness to be kept free and aloof from mercenary considerations; and Plato may fairly urge that he who professes to make his pupils virtuous and good, ought to rely on such goodness for reward, without subjecting the objects of his care to a formal tie of payment. The relation of the moral teacher to the taught is, after all, not a commercial one; its value is not to be estimated in money, but only in

---

[1] See Xenoph. Mem. I. 2, 6.
[2] "Others," says Mr. Mill, " can instruct; but Plato is one of those who form great men by the combination of moral enthusiasm with logical discipline."

form of a return of the same kind and quality as the advantages given,—a moral one that is, a feeling of reverence and gratitude akin to that entertained towards parents or gods; for a paid teacher cannot quite fulfil the part of a self-devoted and entirely disinterested one, any more than a hired governess or nurse can fully replace a parent. And however inapplicable such scrupulosity in practice, it must be admitted to be abstractedly right, and even essential that the character of the teacher and the qualitative standard of the educator should be maintained on the highest possible footing; since a technical proficiency for getting on in life is sure to be in demand, and the empiric is safe whatever becomes of the scientific physician. The difficulty is with those departments of virtue and knowledge which are not showy or ostensibly self-rewarding, where the advantage is distant, visible only to those seeing over the heads of the multitude, and by a light different from that directing the proceedings of ordinary life. Mr. Grote allows that both descriptions of educational activity— the paid and unpaid, or the theoretical and practical —are indispensable to the proper intellectual outfit of of every society; and it may be conceded on the other side that all education on a large scale must necessarily be a sort of drill under official superintendence, limited to certain tangible rudimentary acquirements; but these ought not to be regarded as final or sufficient, or be ranked as of equal value with disinterested tuition of a higher kind; the educational drudge should rather follow the lead of the philosopher—giving life to mechanical routine by the influences of a loftier spirit, so as to awaken a kindred feeling of enthusiasm in the mind of the learner, and maintain the permanent vitality of the teaching.

One especial characteristic of all honest and effectual teaching is that knowledge should lead and ignorance follow; whereas the dishonest teaching usually indicated by the term "sophistry" especially reveals itself in allowing ignorance to take the lead, or at least to react disastrously on the integrity of the lesson, so as to make it rather a reflection of the pupil's own notions and prejudices, a vehicle of what he is prepared for and wishes to hear than of anything else.[1] The Sophist achieves his end not by shewing men how to become wiser or better, but by conforming to their opinions, ministering to their desires, and making them better satisfied with themselves, their deficiencies, and natural propensities, than they

[1] "A popular speaker," said the *Times* (Dec. 6, 1862), "must not be too original; if he is, he becomes unintelligible to his hearers, and in fact disappoints them, because they go expecting and desiring to hear the ordinary recognised views, and to have their own opinions reflected from the mouth of another, so as to return home comfortably self-complacent and self-satisfied." On another occasion (November 1, 1867) the same paper thus described the incompatibility of the politician and the true educator:—"There are and must be those whose function it is to carry some great cause or to work some sweeping reform. They are often great and good men; but as soon as a man has assumed this character his career as a statesman is ended."

were before. A striking instance of this was recently afforded by the conduct of the Ritual Commissioners (1867), who instead of exercising a free judgment on the matter referred to them, thought their duty to consist in submissively appealing to fanciful opinion and the spontaneous tastes and preferences of congregations, referring to this precarious standard alone as their guide, and passing over in silence the profound and far more important questions underlying the childish pantomime of stoles and chasubles. This unworthy attitude of the Sophist is particularly described by Plato in the Gorgias and in the sixth book of the Republic, where adverting to those mercenary teachers who are all things to all men, condescending to flatter vulgar opinion by obsequious repetitions of its own ideas; employing the savoury Mephistophilean device adapted to please every palate, though turning into infernal fire if accidentally spilt upon the touchstone of truth. It seems unaccountable to find Mr. Grote and others openly justifying this style of acquiescent teaching, as if the best teachers were the most popular ones, and as if no blame attached to those who, professing to instruct, only confirm an intrinsically vicious society in its own vicious or imperfect ideas. The more liberal sort of education described above as "sophistical" in a general sense rapidly degenerates under this unfaithful management until it sinks into a narrow denominational teaching, accepting as true and good what is arbitrarily deemed to be such by the particular sects or parties using it for their own purposes; so that the moral vision becomes at last entirely distorted, and the real Sophist appears to be not so much the individual teacher or preacher as the general public or special faction or segment of it employing and directing his services. And where once the moral firmness of the teacher has given way to a craving for popularity, there may occur a reaction of class prejudice or ignorance to any conceivable extent; from moderate concession or "accommodation," down to the craziest perversion of sentiment and the basest betrayal of truth.[1] When, for instance, Dr. Pusey lately pleaded in letters to *The Times*[2] that "the clergy exist not for themselves but for the people;" that "the people don't want to be differently taught;" and that "the liberty of the clergy means the slavery of the people;"—it was impossible not to see that the plea thus ostensibly put forward on the people's behalf was really an apology for the indolence and hypocrisy of the clergy in availing

---

[1] "Professional men, high or low, are mainly kept to their duty by vigilance and intelligence in those dealing with them. At least there is too often a germ of selfishness and craft which unthinking folly in the customer naturally fosters into maturity. Shopkeepers in general are what their customers make them; governments what nations make them. If buyers and subjects are thoughtless, indifferent, or ignorant, sellers and governments will scarcely teach them better. —*The Times*, Oct. 31, 1867.

[2] In February and March, 1868.

themselves of popular ignorance for the easier perpetuation of their own influence and power. The teacher who in this way suppresses a truth or varnishes a statement out of deference to his audience, makes himself an accomplice in their self-deception, by giving to their ignorant surmises the stamp of his own authority.

But plain speaking is often repulsive, and we are admonished as to the necessity of using language allowed and understood by the people. Language and illustration must, as conventional symbols, have a certain form, and with this a certain portion of error inevitably mingles. To this it is of course necessary to submit, so far as it represents an inevitable condition of human utterance; the function of the human mind is that of minister and interpreter, not that of professor or master of the truth; and so long as it faithfully interprets its results in their best available expression no more can be expected of it. But the limit of allowable compliance is passed when it designedly stops short of a full disclosure, or distorts the explanation in deference to the perverse notions of ill-educated hearers. Equally reprehensible is every prostitution of the function of the teacher for an ignoble purpose; and it seems singular that while Plato stipulates in his model Republic for the employment of the highest forms of literature and art, excluding even the most illustrious of Greek poets as too unveracious in his imagery to suit the requirements of harmonious souls, we adopt the opposite plan of pandering to the low tastes of ill-educated readers, the manufacturers of phantasms and literary unreality compounding a continually baser sort of intellectual nutriment for the swinish multitude, calculated as a Circæan cup to enfeeble their souls, and to keep them swine for ever, by preventing their developing into a better kind of animal. The Biblical dictum as to "milk for babes" may be carried too far, especially in these days of food adulteration, and we should remember how St. Paul's unfortunate saying about "being all things to all men" became, under ecclesiastical management, an excuse for that *fraus pia* of which the church has at all times so largely availed itself. In this way the experienced facilities afforded by what is called "accommodation" have induced defenders of the extreme theory of inspiration to ascribe the same sort of politic management to the providence of God, making God responsible for human errors; an inference scarcely to be avoided by those who, like Dr. Alford in his commentary on the New Testament, would fain unite the doctrine of plenary inspiration with the duties of impartial criticism. Such, indeed, is the general tendency of dogmatical theology, which, abandoning the control of rea-

INTRODUCTION. 47

son, leads to what the Germans call the headlong plunge of indiscriminate belief. "We cannot know the absolute," it is said, "therefore we ought to believe,"—(not the most rational beliefs accepted by philosophy), but the crotchets inherited by opinion from tradition; the very theory which in the ninth century formulated the dogma of transubstantiation, and which in all ages has been active in transplanting the rank growths of popular credulity into the garner of the Church.

The eager justification of the Sophists heard simultaneously from so many quarters indicates the prevalence of a strong sympathy and affinity with them, naturally combining with a desire for self-justification; and unfortunately there are plenty of indications that the race of illusory image-makers and unscrupulous teachers of unreality and non-entity is by no means extinct; we see them in the press, the platform, and the pulpit;—like Autolycus, whose revenue was the silly cheat, they avow the intention to condescend to the lowest levels of vulgar credence to win popularity,[1] displaying their tinsel wares of decorous crotchet or wanton artifice in a thousand forms;—whether counterfeiting candour in skilfully balanced assertions, or frittering away a true general

[1] Δημοσίᾳ μακροῖς λόγοις πρὸς πλήθη δυνατὸν εἰρωνεύεσθαι.
—*Sophist.* 268ᵇ.
Anglicè—One able to play the hypocrite in long-winded speeches.

idea in fabulous details, or forcibly delineating one side of a theory or question while partially or entirely suppressing the other. Indeed Mr. Mill, in his above-cited review of Grote, deprecatingly suggests that "to condemn the Sophists were to condemn all popular teaching and all literature. Plato's reprobation," he says, "would reach the most approved teachers of the present day; the established clergy, bribed to profess an existing set of opinions whether believing them or not,—the ministers of non-established sects, the lawyers, the schoolmasters, the teachers and governors of universities, who must all either renounce their profession, or teach what is acceptable to those who listen to them. Statesmen have renounced even the pretence of giving the public anything but what it wishes for; the press, especially that most influential part of it, the public journals, incessantly displays its eagerness to court public opinion, and instead of disagreeable truth, to ply it with things which it likes to hear." This is true, but then it is self-condemnatory, not a justification of the Sophist; the very inference, in fact, to which most men had already come, namely, that the tone of our public teaching, both ecclesiastical and lay, is misleading and insincere, ill suited to "make a hedge for the people to stand the onset of battle in the day of the Lord;" a source of weakness which must be eventually fatal to the policy of a

INTRODUCTION. 49

nation affecting self-government, and so essentially dependent on the widest diffusion of accurate ideas. But the partial currency of deceptive estimates seems an inevitable result of an imperfect education and corrupt society,—affording protection and security to iniquity and falsehood, whose poison, long rankling unseen, becomes afterwards manifested in its effects, and so "curses," as Shakespeare says,[1] the society harbouring it; while in the meantime—

"Authority bears a credent bulk
That no particular scandal once can touch,"

so that at last it seems as if increasing corruption were a necessary adjunct of all artificial society, and the thoughts of philanthropists, like Plato or Rousseau, turn to the possibility of reform through a reconstruction placing it on a more natural footing.

But this proposed reconstruction, in Plato's view at least, is itself subordinate to the moral improvement of individuals; its object being that the State should act as an education, and be as a natural organism bringing forth good fruit in the form of good men.[2] And Mr. Grote would have

[1] Measure for Measure, Act 3, sc. 2.
[2] Plato's first Alcibiades, p. 134ᵇ. Also Aristotle, Eth. Nicom. 2, 1:
—'Οι νομοθέται τοὺς πολίτας ἐθίζοντες ποιοῦσιν ἀγαθούς' καὶ διαφέ.
ρει τούτῳ πολιτεία πολιτείας, ἀγαθὴ φαύλης. Ibid. 1, 10,—Περὶ ἀρετῆς
ἐπισκεπτέον, τάχα γὰρ ὄντως ἂν βέλτιον περὶ τῆς εὐδαιμονίας θεω-
ρήσαιμεν. δοκεῖ δ' ὁ κατ' ἀλήθειαν πολιτικὸς περὶ ταύτην μάλιστα
πεπονῆσθαι. —'Αρετὴν δέ λέγομεν ἀνθρωπίνην οὐ τὴν τοῦ σώματος
ἀλλα τὴν τῆς ψυχῆς, καὶ τὴν εὐδαιμονίαν δὲ ψυχῆς ἐνέργειαν.

4

a better right to call Plato prejudiced and unpractical had he himself pointed out a better way of effecting a similar purpose, instead of ridiculing the notion of treating walls, clocks, ships as trivialities[1] in comparison with the paramount aim of forming good citizens. It is for the politician schooled exclusively in the empirical philosophy of the last two centuries, and on that foundation treating the State as a mere mechanism acting as a police force protecting one immoral unit against another, to deal with the question of reform as one of mere structural change or revolution; whereas the Platonist would treat it rather as a resuscitation of the moral qualities of its human members, or the making men good through the best educational agencies, fortifying the irresolute will, and for this end facilitating the prompt exposure of insidious deception whenever it ventures to show itself. For such a one it was pleasant to read on a late occasion the instantaneous exposure of a mendacious plea for Ritualism based on the characteristic breadth and liberality of the English Church; complimenting, in fact, the intended dupe on his superior magnanimity, and making liberalism the stalking-horse of the grossest illiberalism.[2] The refutation reaches beyond the particular

---

[1] Grote's History, vol. viii. p. 538.
[2] See the *Pall Mall Gazette*, Sept. 3, 1867. The late catholic protest against the language used by Garibaldi at Geneva was also uttered in the name of liberty; *i.e.* the liberty to wear chains of the worst description.

case, applying to all Protestant capitulation to an absolutist Church ; but it is of course more especially needed where the pretext is used to mask a fraudulent device, and to set up a domineering infallibility in the disguise of a liberal establishment.

"Can philosophy do without religion?" lately asked an astute bishop, "Can democracy subsist without God?"[1] Assuredly not, but then it is not sectarian indoctrination or blind submission to tradition from which safety and stability can be anticipated; the laws and discipline of churches are by no means the expression of the "wisdom from on high" to which the Bishop appealed; rather may each advance made by churches in specifying dogmas and details of obligation be accounted a step in demoralisation, superseding free agency by priestly direction, and obscuring the divine order by artificial regulations. And when the Bishop went on to plead for ecclesiasticism against philosophy, on the ground of the discrepancies of philosophic systems, he suppressed the fact that these discrepancies, arising from the one-sided views of sincere enquirers, tend to become ever less in the progress of investigation; whereas the differences of churches,[2] being founded

---

[1] *Times*, October 10, 1867.
[2] The church fallacy may be succinctly disposed of by a simple consideration of the nature of morality and of a moral person. A person is a free agent, having rights and obligations; moral obligation is the allegiance owed by such a person to the divine order. Now a church

on artificial conventionality and unreason, grow perpetually greater through the disintegrating powers constantly undermining their stability, until they eventually split down to the unitary soul, where alone the hope of rational reconstruction is to be found.[1]

No doubt churches achieve a temporary precarious unity of a certain sort, but only through the blind faith or indolent subserviency of their members; but irrepressible reason only awaits a fitting opportunity to rebel—a crisis often precipitated by the mischievously felt results of the union of morbid theory and party feeling which it is sure to engender. There is, indeed, a striking analogy between Church unions and the Trade unions lately so much discussed; and saw-grinders ethics may quote venerable precedents in the intolerant ecclesiastical

professing divine authority interposes its own regulations in place of universal order, and supersedes free agency by priestly direction;—in short it suppresses God and man, leaving only its own corrupt incompetent self surviving. This of course refers only to the corporate action of churches, not to the salutary efforts of many clergymen considered as individuals, who are generally far better than the system to which they are compelled to conform.

[1] Church education is necessarily drill, because churches depend on the favour of the multitude, the passive inheritor of a routine derived from remote and barbarous ages. The Bishop of Glocester and Bristol lately (Thursday, October 24th, 1867) proposed the following antidotes for dissent: First, To pray for strength to show greater earnestness in the work; secondly, To remain strictly true to our own Church system, a "fixity of principle" which he said was "attractive to the conscientious dissenter;"—in other words the old plan of *sound* doctrine to be unalterably maintained in defiance of objection, and furnishing a welcome *point d'appui* to those who are too impatient to suspend their judgment, or too ignorant or indolent to judge at all.

practices of former ages. These were based on a similar distortion of moral sentiment, originating pretensions and acts astonishing as well as repulsive to those outside the magic circle. All artificial association narrower than the great natural one tends in a greater or less degree to suggest narrow views, and to turn the notion of obligation in the direction of special interest; while the very fact of speciality, by intercepting wider and more impartial estimates, renders such ostensible obligations profoundly immoral. The immorality is certainly more flagrant where appearing as mere individual selfishness; but the selfishness of classes, cliques, commercial companies, etc., is scarcely less obnoxious,[1] while far more insidiously misleading, because here the inherent immorality is veiled by a semblance of public spirit and an approximation to unselfish generality, although, in fact, constituting a conspiracy against the general; and though under apt management they might, in addition to the special purposes of the particular league, be made educationally instrumental towards gaining truer and more perfect notions of the general, the imperfect moral condition

[1] The so styled "educational reform" of the present day is after all only an effort for a better sort of Sophistical education, a plea for useful instruction or liberal accomplishment in opposition to the routine teaching of cliques, churches, and classes—those "solid existences" lately described by the *Times* (December 2nd, 1867) as holding the keys of education in their hands, and resolutely determined to continue to hold them against all comers. Education is in short the property or prerogative of self-interested parties.

of their members usually operates in practice to obscure the true nature of obligation, and to reduce such associations to mere schools of selfishness.

In none of the recent discussions about education (so far as known to the writer) has the subject been largely and worthily treated; on each occasion more stress is laid on form than matter, and again on the matter rather than on the spirit of the teaching;—this being always represented as something to be externally laid on, or "given," in sophistical fashion, the only doubt being as to the sort of trowel with which it should be applied, whether it ought to be voluntary or compulsory, secular, denominational, or mixed. But even the question as to what ought to to be thus "given," or "what it is of most importance that the people should know," is not to be met, as lately attempted in the brilliant but somewhat flashy oration of Mr. Lowe,[1] by flippant remarks upon the discrepancies of metaphysical systems, or wholesale disparagement of ancient literature and old things generally, since all human development is continuous, and the old offers in many respects the best means of estimating the value and reason of the new. It is, indeed, the great fault of the English mind to bow submissively to custom and tradition, without any discriminating reference to circumstances and antecedents, or the possible reasons for its continu-

[1] *Times*, November 4, 1867.

ance or disuse. Few will dispute the proposition that plough-boys are unfit subjects for Latin grammar; but it does not follow from this, or because grammar may have been neglected by the Romans, that it is useless now, any more than that ethnology should be dropped because neglected by Esquimaux, or zoology, because unshared by its unconscious subjects in the Regent's Park. "Language grew," says Mr. Lowe, "it was not made by grammatical rules;" but so do plants and trees; they owe nothing to Lindley or Linnæus; and yet, though sharing the imperfections of all biological science, the science of botany is studied with advantage. The disparagement of literature as an educational instrument may easily recoil upon science, if we reflect how true science is essentially active and progressive; whereas, applied as an instrument of rudimentary education, it can only be dogmatical information in the dry, unfruitful form of summaries of results, to be either passively gazed at as seen in experimental illustrations, or mechanically committed to memory;—a painful effort to form out of tissues of old hypotheses a perennial vesture for the intellect, ending only in the production of a net which hampers its movements while making its essential nudity ridiculously conspicuous. For that boys can be got or "led" by their teachers to rediscover for themselves independently the known laws of nature, can only be regarded as an amiable hallucination, yet one very natural to the enthusiastic man of science, who sees around his lecture-table the eager faces of boys animated with delight, not so much indeed at the laws as at the lovely gewgaws which it is his mission to exhibit. The advocates of science in schools consider the great end of education to be the "sharpening of the intellect,"—undervaluing or forgetting the educational influences of art, and that in individual souls, as in general history, the cultivation of a feeling for the beautiful is the best and most natural prelude to the study of the true. Mr. Lowe intimates the education of a German waiter to be superior to that of an Oxford first-class man, and the advantage of knowing a modern language to be principally shewn by the facilities afforded by it in ordering dinner at a café. He advocates a low utilitarian standard, in seeming disregard of higher utilities, as where dwelling on the "felicity of expression"[1] to be met with in French or Greek, while omitting the uses of these languages for the study of history and philosophy. But it is not a question of mere elegance of style, or even the practical conveniences of a universal language, in some degree answered by Latin; the spirit

---

[1] "Others for language all their care express,
And value books, as women men, for dress—
Their praise is still—the style is excellent!"

of ideal beauty, justice, and true humanity ennobles ancient literature, and there is an absence of affectation as well as of dogmatical prejudice which is scarcely elsewhere to be found. Certainly it is no revolutionary feeling in the speaker which prompts disparagement of the classics, but rather the instinctive impulse of the orator to feed the prejudices of his audience. In this sense the address was well suited to flatter the self-complacency of ill-educated persons naturally incapable of understanding the value of what they have not; but the wholesale depreciation of moral philosophy and metaphysics is ill justified by the fact of English neglect. It had been less sophistically plausible perhaps, but more really useful to have pointed out the causes and consequences of this neglect; how leading to an undignified utilitarianism and the abandonment of the highest human interests to the management of churches; and originating in the characteristic ecclesiastical jealousy by which, reversing the better tendencies of the Socratic period, the secular study of these sciences was in former ages discredited and suppressed. It is, indeed, in his imperfect acquaintance with these sciences that the Englishman especially fails, becoming in consequence a prey to all sorts of hallucinations and misconceptions in the respective departments, mistaking mere fashion for morality, and possessing no solid or rational assurance of having a soul at all. Nor, according to certain recent utterances, can any interest be supposed to attach to the problem, except so far as a man requires "a sharp and bright instrument" or tool to enable him to "advance in life and to transact business;" hence the derisively added words—"a man may be expected to be a sort of gardener to his mind;" yet if he have a mind, his mind must be emphatically himself, and in that case it were better to be gardener to his mind than to merge his whole mind in the shoemaker or gardener. Mr. Lowe says, we ought to know, above all, "those transactions out of which the present state of our political and social relations have arisen." But for this purpose ancient history is as needful as modern. If the first memorable example of freedom was given by Greece, while Rome shewed what could be effected on a large scale by organisation and legal institution, the histories of those nations can never become obsolete or unimportant for educational purposes, especially if it be considered that each of them impresses a serious negative as well as a positive lesson, exemplifying in its decline the fatal consequences of the lack of the quality more especially cultivated by the other. How can the pretensions of the Papacy, or the motives of the municipalities, nationalities, and laws of Modern Europe, be adequately comprehended except in their relation to a prior state of things, in which too many of the special usages of modern nations, religious and otherwise, as well as their theology and speculative philosophy, originated? The very subject which most of all incurs Mr. Lowe's ridicule, namely the heathen mythology, seems, in this respect, most especially to deserve our study,—that throughout the period best known through the commonly read Greek literature, it was in a perpetual state of inevitable decline, an obsolete symbolism tenacious indeed of life, and hanging to existence by many ties of vested interest and ignorant credulity, yet constantly tending to obliteration with the advance of culture in the interests of a better religion of morality and philosophy. Even the antique symbolism itself, in its various stages of fetichism, anthropomorphism, and philosophical interpretation, may claim to make an important part of modern study, as immediately illustrative of important changes now in progress; not, indeed, as ordinarily set forth by pragmatical historians, or in school books and "manuals of question and answer," but as taught by Vico, Heyne, Buttmann, and many others, as a record of the inevitable vicissitudes of inexperienced opinion, and as a light thrown by the most ancient history of the world on some of the most valued books and most prominent mental phenomena of the present day.

In estimating the Platonic quarrel with the

Sophists, Mr. Grote misses the gist of the controversy,—all important as it is even to the politician,—namely, the elimination of the true notion of education, considered as a mental edifice to be raised on political and dialectical foundations; first, by the formation of good habits through social training, and next, through the further philosophic training of individual minds to a condition of moral autonomy. From this educational point of view the general weal becomes relatively subordinate to that of the individual, and Mr. Grote, from not perceiving this, is betrayed into the error of supposing the "Ethical End" to be better apprehended by the Platonic Protagoras than by Socrates himself;[1] whose politics, unconfined to local interests and particular societies, look to ideal harmony and perfection as a virtually religious end to be sought through individual improvement. Only in this sense can the determination of the best standard or most desirable educational quality be properly referred to the social status, meaning man's place in the order of the universe; and this is only saying in other words that the aim of education should be to form a truly moral life. The Gospel here reinforces Plato in propounding an ideal life, or spiritual perfection, as the end of human effort, an aim which, though seeming but emptiness or revolutionary folly to material-

[1] History, vol. viii. p. 517.

istic politicians, borrows from secular politics many pertinent analogies, being itself susceptible of becoming in a sense both wealth and power. In its New Testament representation it appears as a priceless pearl, the one thing needful among many lesser utilities, consisting especially in righteousness or goodness, and this again in a will harmonising with the divine, or, as elsewhere expressed, in sympathetic recognition of the "Spiritual Word," an expression which, considered apart from the formal peculiarities and personal associations of the Gospel in which it occurs, may be translated the manifestation of divine wisdom, or the light and life of the world. The kingdom of heaven in the soul forms the subject of endless evangelical illustration. It is the feast of the halt and maimed,—a distant inheritance, yet so far realised in the present as to be already the joy of the afflicted, the riches of the poor. Originating in seeming non-entity, like the secret fermentation in meal, yet from the smallest of all seeds expanding into the noblest of trees, it is essentially a growth, depending for its fruitfulness on the fertility of the soil and the purity of the food provided for it—often jeopardised by a rank growth of interfering tares, and requiring weeding or even fiery purification; a hidden treasure demanding investment and active cultivation, without which it becomes really the vacuity which to the uninitiated it always appears, falling back into the original nothingness from which apparently it issued.[1] It is built neither on Pharisaic ceremonial nor on the wisdom of the Scribes, nor is it to be considered as won by learning dogmas and hypotheses by rote, or curiously gazing at the "signs and wonders" of the lecture-room; it is rather a new birth, an internal power contemplating and ideally imitating the living operations of creative power, and so increasing in life and energy, whereas sophistry, attaching itself to the husk of dogmas and formulas, becomes enslaved and at last suffocated by its cumbrous unassimilated investiture. The aim of this perhaps too lengthy introduction has been to shew, in opposition to certain recent disparaging commentaries on Plato, the paramount necessity of cultivating the soul's life, or its active and moral capabilities, as popularly set forth in the above Gospel illustrations; of making this the all-influencing aim of education, not in the sense of mere discipline or drill, but as the infusion of a new spirit underlying all superstructures of professional dexterity or sophistical accomplishment; to shew how these commentaries, interesting and able as they are in many respects, fail utterly[2] when approaching the subject of philo-

[1] Matthew xiii. 12.
[2] Thus Mr. Mill says—"The idea of measure as a good in itself, independently of an end beyond it, seems to have grown upon Plato as he advanced in life; but we measure a thing to make it conformable to something else; and Plato does not tell us what that something is." Yet the omission is of no moment in Mr. Mill's view, for he

sophical idealism, by them regarded as "unpractical," but without which, as if without room to expand or a congenial atmosphere, all spiritual life must languish and die. And this is of more especial consequence when we touch the subject of morality, which can have no real existence in ephemeral opinion, or among the economic, physiological, and other miscellaneous lore where casuistical ingenuity professes to find it; and which must continue to baffle and perplex the English mind until, neglecting the superficial nostrums of sophistical advisers, and looking back to the Christian, Socratic, and Kantian teaching, it begins to study itself, and to recognise in that hitherto little explored region the possibilities of a new world. And though the natural law, which is the sage's only law,[1] be not originally written there, a congenial faculty for its discovery will at least be forthcoming; while in

adds—" Scepticism as to the Absolute never did any harm nor made any difference to any human being." Mr. Mill complains (p 287) that no writer of equal merit to Plato leaves us in so much uncertainty as to his real opinions;—the dialogues " exhibit no consistent system." Elsewhere he suggests that the non-solution of difficulties started arose from indifference to truth; and, moreover, that Plato became inconsistent with himself by dogmatising "in his old age;" as if it were not the most natural thing in the world to sum up our knowledge in old age, and as if the more didactic tone of the later dialogues were not to a great extent problematically illustrative and mythical.

[1] C'est en vain qu'on aspire à la liberté sous la sauvegarde des lois. Des lois? Partout tu n'as vu regner sous ce nom que l'interet particulier et les passions des hommes. Mais les lois eternelles de la nature existent. Elles tiennent lieu de loi positive au sage; elles sont écrites au fond de son cœur par la conscience et la raison; c'est à celles-la qu'il faut s'asservir pour être libre.—*Rousseau's Emile*, Bk. 5.

the voluntary appropriation of such a law by means of education lies the germ of that true liberty[1] which belonged to the slave Epictetus, and without which the contest for rights and franchises among the nominally free resembles only the self-defeating struggles of a fly becoming continually more tightly entangled in the meshes of its foe. And this foe, the cunning spinner of sophistical cobwebs, is everywhere at hand, intent with subtle and inexhaustible resources to stifle and extinguish the better influences which might be fatal to his craft; not only by constructing appropriate instrumental apparatus in the way of delusive images and multifarious lures of morbid excitement and frivolous amusement, but more especially by the corruption which is the object of all this machinery, namely by feeding and cherishing the lie-engendering spirit, all that in the way of selfishness, envy, intolerance, ignorance, or self-conceit,—prepares opportunities for deception generally among mankind, and also acts the ever busy sophist within our own souls. How, under such circumstances, can truthful sincerity hope to succeed where Socrates and Jesus failed; how shall the advocate of ideal excellence compete with the champions of popular opinion, or expect to prevail against those whose sole business is to flatter and to please?

[1] Je ris de ces peuples avilis, qui, de laissant ameuter par des ligueurs, osent parler de liberté sans même en avoir l'idée, et qui, le cœur plein de tous les vices des esclaves, s'imaginent que pour être libres il suffit d'être des mutins.—*Rousseau, on the Government of Poland.*

THE SOPHIST.

SYNOPSIS OF THE CONTENTS.

ENUMERATION of various aspects of the Sophist, described under the head of—

1st. Forcibly acquisitive art, as a fisher or angler.

2ndly. Peaceably acquisitive art, as a trafficker in knowledge.

3rdly. Again, as forcibly acquisitive—in public—in the way of disputing or wrangling.

4thly. As a sifter or purifier. This seemingly anomalous aspect perplexes Theætetus, hence the necessity of seeking some farther essential mark reconciling and uniting those before named.

5thly. The Sophist as a word-contender or wrangler, professing to dispute about all manner of things, and to teach others to do the like. This of course can be seriously attempted only in the way of make-believe or imitation.

6thly. But there are two kinds of imitation, assimilative and exact, or unfaithful and fantastic; which of the two should be ascribed to the Sophist is left for the present doubtful.

But how is fantastic or untrue imitation possible? How can falsehood, which is virtual non-entity, be said *to be*, or exist? How affirm that which is not?

This plea urged on behalf of Sophistry, as if in the obnoxious sense it were an imaginary or impossible thing, introduces a long discussion on relative as distinguished from absolute existence, in the course of which the followers of Zeno and Parmenides are shown to have missed the mark. For—

1st. We may admit that the dictum of Parmenides as to the contrariety of being and non-being, each understood in an absolute sense, would in strictness lead to the above perplexing dilemma, and to the sophistical vindication of falsehood deduced from it. It is certainly impossible to speak of falsehood, in the sense of absolute non-entity, without self-contradiction; so that the Sophist, as an image-maker, seems to have here gained an unassailable position; but an image is not absolute non-entity, it is only relatively so, existing as an image or likeness, though not as the thing itself, and in a certain sense mingling and uniting being and non-being.

2ndly. This not being immediately allowed by the Sophist, it becomes necessary to reconsider carefully the whole subject of entity as well as of non-entity, which an historical review of the preceding philosophy shows to have been hitherto very inadequately dealt with; the theories defining it numerically, either as one or as many, are both beset by insuperable difficulty.

3rdly. The same may be said of other customary methods of dealing with it, as those of the materialists and idealists; the former being compelled by the phenomena of life and soul to admit spiritual being, and that true being is best described as *power* to do or suffer;— the latter, who talk of holding communion with movement through our bodies, and with true being through our thoughts, are bound to explain what they mean by the phrase "holding communion;" which in fact can only be a sort of mutual doing and suffering, again leading us to power or force as its origin; a faculty not confined to body, since the soul knows, and knowing and being known are essentially an acting and suffering; the "communion" with real being attributed to thought implies this mutuality, which is necessarily a result of force. Yet it also implies rest, since without stability and repose in real being, science or knowledge were impossible. This contradictory assertion of combined rest and movement leads to a new dilemma.

4thly. Explanation of the seeming antinomies of many and one, rest and movement, etc., in the intellectual sphere, or that of true being, through the doctrine of the intercommunion of ideas, carried on in diversified lines of movement; one leading through their correctly formed connection to greater truth and light, the other through their incorrect Sophistical combination to increasing obscurity and error. The correct association and severance of ideas, like that of letters or of sounds, is the object of a special art, namely that of dialectics; the perverse ingenuity of the Sophist which severs the congruous and unites the inconsistent, is a manipulation of relative, not absolute non-

SYNOPSIS OF THE CONTENTS. 69

entity, through the multifarious byepaths and labyrinthine complications of *the different*.

This is made to appear more clearly in an example. Of the five leading ideas or terms—being, movement, rest, identity, and difference, some unite, some refuse to unite, some unite partially, others generally or universally. Movement is opposed to rest, but both unite with being, since both *are;* movement again is not identity, yet it is an identical thing—*i.e.* considered in itself, and even movement may be said to partake of rest in a certain sense. Movement again is not diversity, yet it partakes of diversity; it is not being, yet it partakes of being; thus non-being passes through all forms; each is, and yet is not, so far as partaking the nature of diversity; each form contains much entity and also an infinite abundance of non-entity (pp. 255, 256). In this sense non-entity may be said *to be*.

The Platonic doctrine here transcends the Elean or Parmenidean, blending with it the essential truth of the Ionian or Heraclitean theory, aad not only affirming non-entity, but showing *how* it may be said to exist. But it ill becomes a true philosopher to take advantage of these antinomies for purposes of mere empty display or cavilling disputation (p. 259); since an arbitrary severance of all ideas as well as their perverse intermixture must be destructive to all reasoning. Reasoning or discourse is the correct association of ideas. But non-entity, as already said, extends through all forms of being; and if it be capable of mingling and associating with opinion and discourse, error and false reasoning may easily ensue. Error and falsehood lead to illusion and deception; and so the world becomes full of misleading imagery. This was the very point at which we before left the Sophist,—protesting that according to the deliberate dicta of venerable philosophers, it is impossible to think or speak non-entity,—to which is now added the objection that opinion and discourse are not among the number of forms with which nonentity mingles. A refutation of this objection convicting the Sophist of being a wordy imitator or mimic of the real in conformity with the general argument extends to p. 264c.

It remains only to consider whether the Sophist belongs to the class of faithful and exact image-makers, or the fantastic class,—distinguished at p. 236c from the other. Here we are referred back to the initial distinction of all art into acquisitive and creative (p. 219); since imitation is a creation of imagery; creative art is either divine or human, each creating images as well as things. Human imagery is, as before stated, either faithful or fantastic; the latter may be effected either by borrowed instrumentality or through the personal resources of the individual; by one knowing what he imitates, *i.e.* the true philosopher—or by one only appearing to know; and this either in an ignorant supposition that he does know, or else deliberately and consciously pretending to a knowledge which he has not. Of this last sort, some are stump orators or public speakers; others exhibiting their insincere ironical pretensions in private discourses, are the Sophists.

The prominent part here assigned to the Elean Stranger, while Socrates remains silent, is probably owing to the consideration that the refutation of the purely dialectical fallacies combated in the dialogue had been less dramatically appropriate in the mouth of one whose aim was mainly ethical, and more especially in order to indicate that in Plato's opinion the Elean or Parmenidean doctrine, understood with due qualification and in its most legitimate development, did not really warrant the overstrained and perverse inferences drawn from it by some of its professed adherents.

THE SOPHIST.

THEODORUS, SOCRATES, AN ELEAN STRANGER,
THEÆTETUS.

THEOD.—Conformably to our yesterday's agreement, Socrates, we have come ourselves and have brought with us this stranger, by birth an Elean, one of the followers of Parmenides and Zeno, and a great philosopher.

SOCR.—Possibly, Theodorus, you have unconsciously brought with you not a mere mortal visitor, but a God; since Homer tells how Gods—the God of strangers especially—are wont, in company with just and conscientious persons, to come inspecting the iniquities and righteousness of men. So perhaps this stranger is some higher being who has followed you in order to inspect and impeach the imperfections of our reasonings, being, in truth, some cross-examining God.

THEOD.—Not so, Socrates; our friend's argumentative method is, comparatively speaking, temperate and moderate;[1] and though the man, in my opinion, is no God, he has nevertheless something divine about him; for such, indeed, I hold to be the case with all true philosophers.

Socr.—You do well, my friend; although I fear that this kind of man is not much easier to distinguish than that of the Gods. For these,—I mean the true, not fictitious, philosophers,—assume all sorts of fictitious semblances through others' ignorance, and in the course of their peregrinations and inspection of the life of those below them, appear to some nothing worth, while surpassingly excellent in the esteem of others. Sometimes they take the form of statesmen, sometimes of (teachers or) sophists, while to some they seem as if altogether insane. However, I would gladly learn from this our guest, if not displeasing to him, what opinion his countrymen entertain, and what name they give to these several characters.

Theod.—What characters?

Socr.—Those of the Sophist, the politician, and the philosopher.[2]

Theod.—What specific doubt respecting them prompts your inquiry?

---

[1] That is, compared with other dialecticians of the same school.

[2] The entire subject would consequently be disposed of by adding to the present dialogue a translation of the Theætetus and Politicus, with illustrations to the former from the Parmenides and Philebus.

Socr.—I wish to know whether they esteem them as one, or as two, or as three, assigning each of the three names to a separate genus.

Theod.—There can, I presume, be no objection to answer the question;—how say you, Stranger?

Strang.—None in the least, Theodorus; there is neither scruple nor difficulty in saying that they consider them to be three; at the same time, to define each of them accurately is no small or easy task.

Theod.—You have accidentally, Socrates, touched on matters which we happened to be questioning him about before coming here, and he then made the same answer to us as now to you, saying he has heard and recollects all about it.

Socr.—Do not then, Stranger, refuse the favour already asked. Tell us first, however, this—whether you prefer to reply in the form of a continuous discourse, or rather in that of answers to a series of questions, the form in which once, when young, I remember hearing Parmenides deliver some very beautiful arguments, he being very old at the time?

Strang.—The colloquial form is certainly better, if it be used fluently and easily; if not, the form of monologue were preferable.

Socr.—Choose, then, among those present one with whom to converse, for all will readily follow you. But if you take my advice you will select one of the younger men—Theætetus here, for instance, or any other you like.

Strang.—I feel ashamed, Socrates, at having in this, our first interview, to hold a lengthened discourse, either alone or with another, as if to make a display; for, in truth, the subject proposed is not to be comprised in a simple answer to a question as one might think, but is a matter requiring long discussion. Yet not to comply with your and their wishes were rude and unfriendly, especially after what you have said; and I accept Theætetus as my fellow dialogist the more readily because I was already conversing with him in anticipation of your recommendation.

Theæt.—Pray do then, Stranger, consent to gratify us all?

Strang.—Say no more, Theætetus; I shall now address myself to you; and if hereafter you should feel fatigue through the prolixity of what you undertake, you must not blame me, but your own friends here.

Theæt.—I don't fear defeat this time; but, in case of accident, I will take this younger Socrates, a crony of my own age, as an ally—one who is not unaccustomed to share my exercises.

Strang.—Well! settle this between yourselves as the discourse proceeds. We will begin, then, our mutual enquiry with the Sophist: considering and explaining what he is. At present you and I have only the name in common; each of us probably entertains a different idea as to the thing. But in every matter it is far more important to be agreed as to the thing by means of rational explanations, than to repeat the name without explanation. Now, it is not easy to determine the class or kind in which the Sophist is to be placed. But since, in order to deal effectually with great and important matters, universal experience shews it to be better to approach the investigation by means of simple and easy examples, I propose that we should do so in the present case, and study the obscure nature of the Sophist and his mode of action in some familiar instance; unless you, Theætetus, can point out a better way.

THEÆT.—I can think of none better.

STRANG.—Suppose then we take something common and trivial, using it as a pattern or illustration of a greater thing.

THEÆT.—Well!

STRANG.—Let us take something easily manageable and familiar, yet admitting rational exposition as much as a greater,—a fisherman, for instance; this is a well-known and common thing.

THEÆT.—Certainly.

STRANG.—I think it may suggest a method and an explanation not inapposite to our purpose.

THEÆT.—Then will it answer well.

STRANG.—Come, then, let us begin thus: shall we call the fisherman an artist; or inartistic, but possessing some other faculty.

THEÆT.—Certainly not inartistic!

STRANG.—But all art falls under two kinds.

THEÆT.—How so?

STRANG.—Agriculture and all manipulations of material body,—the putting together and forming of utensils, and the imitative art, all these may be called by one name.

THEÆT.—What name?

STRANG.—When one brings into existence that which before had no existence, then we say that he who does so makes, and that the thing so brought into being is made or created.

THEÆT.—Right.

STRANG.—But all the above-recited arts have a power of effecting this.

THEÆT.—They have.

STRANG.—Summing them altogether in one, we may call them creative art ($\pi o\iota\eta\tau\iota\kappa\acute{\eta}$).

THEÆT.—Yes.

STRANG.—On the other hand, all the operations of science and knowledge, of money-making, gymnastics, hunting, etc.,—these, as creating nothing new, but only taking hold of things existing already, in the way of apprehending them by acts or words, or preventing others doing so, may be called acquisitive art (κτητική).

THEÆT.—Just so.

STRANG.—All art, then, being either creative or acquisitive, in which class shall we place the art of fishing?

THEÆT.—Doubtless in the acquisitive class.

STRANG.—But is not the acquisitive art itself of two kinds: one carried on by voluntary interchanges of gifts, wages, and values; the other, a seizure by means of acts or words altogether forcibly?

THEÆT.—So it appears.

STRANG.—But is not the forcibly acquisitive art too susceptible of two-fold division?

THEÆT.—How?

STRANG.—One kind consisting in open competition, the other in secret hunting.

THEÆT.—Yes.

STRANG.—But the art of hunting too we must needs in reason divide.

THEÆT.—Say how.

STRANG.—Into hunting the inanimate, and hunting the animate.

THEÆT.—Of course, if there are both these.

STRANG.—Of course there must be; and we must 220 leave alone the hunting of the inanimate, which, for the most part, is nameless, unless it be the art of diving and such like; on the other hand, we will call the art of hunting the animate—animal hunting.

THEÆT.—Be it so.

STRANG.—Of animal hunting again there may be said to be two sorts: one hunting on dry land, of which there are several kinds and names; another, the hunting of sailing and floating animals, or liquid hunting.

THEÆT.—Certainly.

STRANG.—Of the floating animals, some are in air, some in water.

THEÆT.—Certainly.

STRANG.—The hunting of the feathered tribe is called fowling.

THEÆT.—True.

STRANG.—And the aquatic hunting is almost wholly fishing.

THEÆT.—Yes.

STRANG.—But say, shall we not divide this sort of hunting also into two chief parts?

THEÆT.—What parts?

STRANG.—One sort carried on with nets or gins, the other with blows.

THEÆT.—How do you distinguish each?

STRANG.—One, because everything enclosing and constraining another may be called a barrier or net.

THEÆT.—Certainly.

STRANG.—Such contrivances, whether formed of

THE SOPHIST. 79

wicker or twine, or nooses of reeds or drags, are they not all snares or nets?

THEÆT.—Doubtless.

STRANG.—This sort of hunting then we may term net hunting, or something of the sort.

THEÆT.—Yes.

STRANG.—But the hunting with hooks and spears or by a blow, we may call hunting by striking, or can you suggest a better name?

THEÆT.—Never mind the name; this is quite good enough.[1]

STRANG.—But of the hunting by blows some is carried on by night with torches, so that the fishing is called torch fishing.

[1] The throwing out a network of generalisation or hypothesis is the first step towards the construction of science, and Mr. Grote (Plato, vol. ii, p. 402) points out the importance, in Plato's time, of these examples of systematic classification and analysis, when as yet there were no treatises on logic, nor any clearly recognised course of mental procedure. It were gratuitous to suppose here a satirical allusion to the pedantic hair-splitting practised by contemporary Sophists (Ibid. p. 407 note). "The positive aim of the Platonic dialectics," says Mr. Mill (Essays, 3, p. 321) "is the direct search for the common feature of things classed together, in other words, the meaning of the class-name. It comprehends the processes of definition and division, the systematic employment of which was a new thing in Plato's day. They are indissolubly connected, division being the only road to definition. To find what a thing is it is necessary to set out from being in general, or from some large and known kind, including the thing sought; to dismember this into its component parts, and these again into others, each division being, if possible, only into two members, (an anticipation of Ramus and Bentham) marking at each stage the distinctive feature differentiating one member from the other. By the time we have divided down to the thing sought, we have remarked its points of agreement with all the things to which it is allied, and also those constituting its differences; and are thus enabled to produce a definition of it which is a compendium of its whole nature.

THEÆT.—So it is.

STRANG.—But that by day may be all called hook fishing, since the spears too which are used in it are barbed or hooked.

THEÆT.—So they say.

STRANG.—But of the hunting by blows of hooks one sort is practised from above, downwards, and is called spearing or harpooning.

THEÆT.—So indeed they call it.

STRANG.—And there remains one kind only, in which the hook, unlike the harpoon, does not strike any part of the body at random, but always some part of the mouth or head, and by means of a reed or rod draws the fish from below upwards. Now what name, Theætetus, shall we give to this operation?

THEÆT.—I think we have now solved the problem which it was proposed to unravel.

STRANG.—You and I, then, are now agreed not only as to the name of the art of angling, but as to the thing. For of all art one-half was acquisitive, the half of this seizing, half of this hunting, half of this animal hunting, half of this hunting in a fluid, —the lower division of which was the fisherman's art; of fishing half was fishing by blows, half again of this hook fishing; and the half of this which draws from below upwards is the angler's art, which has obtained a name[1] in analogy with the action practised.

---

[1] Ἀσπαλιευτική

THEÆT.—This is certainly very sufficiently explained.

STRANG.—Come now, let us endeavour to find out according to this example what a Sophist is.

THEÆT.—Very well.

STRANG.—In conformity with our plan we have to enquire first, whether the angler be an ignoramus or possessor of art?

THEÆT.—Certainly not an ignoramus; I understand your meaning, namely, that one having the name of "Sophist" should possess the thing to which the name applies; but what particular art are we to suppose him to possess?

STRANG.—What art? has it then escaped us that the two men we have been talking of have affinity with one another?

THEÆT.—Which men?

STRANG.—Why the angler and the Sophist.

THEÆT.—How so?

STRANG.—Both appear to me to be hunters.

THEÆT.—What then is the game of the Sophist? of the other enough has been said.

STRANG.—Did we not just now divide hunting into fluid hunting and land hunting?

THEÆT.—Yes.

STRANG.—And that portion of the whole which has to do with floating in water we have already explained; the land hunting we left undivided, remarking only that it comprehends many kinds.

222   Theæt.—Yes.

Strang.—So far then the Sophist and angler both proceed from a common art of acquiring.

Theæt.—So it appears.

Strang.—But in their animal hunting they separate, one turning to the sea, the rivers and lakes, the other to the land, and to certain other rivers, inexhaustible pastures as it were of wealth and youth, in order to get hold of the animals there nourished.

Theæt.—How mean you?

Strang.—Of the land hunting there were two great divisions.

Theæt.—Which?

Strang.—One the hunting of tame, the other of wild animals.

Theæt.—Are tame animals then hunted?

Strang.—Yes; if man be a tame animal. But make what supposition you like: either that there is no tame animal, or that some other animal is tame and man wild; or will you suppose man to be tame, but not an object of chase. Tell me which supposition you prefer.

Theæt.—I think, my friend, that we are tame animals, and that man is an object of chase.

Strang.—Let us then say that tame animal hunting is of two kinds.

THEÆT.—How so?

STRANG.—All robbery, enslavement, tyranny, and warfare we place under one head of hunting with violence; but judgment, oratory, affability, we may also include in one term as popular conciliation or persuasion.

THEÆT.—Very well.

STRANG.—But of persuasion we may say that there are two sorts; one private, the other public. Of the former again, one kind seeks pay, the other confers gifts.

THEÆT.—I don't follow this.

STRANG.—It seems you have not yet paid attention to the chase carried on by lovers?

THEÆT.—In what respect?

STRANG.—Inasmuch as they confer gifts on the beloved objects.

THEÆT.—True.

STRANG.—Let this then be set apart as the form of the lovers' art.[1] But of the mercenary or pay-seeking subdivision, that kind which courts popular favour, and using pleasure as a bait, seeks only sustenance for self, all men would, I suppose, call the art of pleasing or adulation.

THEÆT.—Certainly.

[1] The subdivision of hunters of individuals by persuasion into two classes, one disinterested and self-sacrificing, the other having profit in view, points to one, though certainly not the only difference between the philosopher and Sophist.

Strang.—But the other kind, professing to court association for the sake of cultivating virtue, yet receiving reward in the shape of pay, does not this deserve a different appellation?

Theæt.—Certainly it does.

Strang.—But what name? Try and tell us.

Theæt.—It is evident. We seem now to have discovered the Sophist: this, I think, is the fitting name for him.

Strang.—So then, according to our present course of reasoning, Theætetus, the Sophistical art is a sort of acquisitive land-animal-hunting, a chase of individual men for money reward, a hunting of rich and noble young men by seeming educators.

Theæt.—Such it certainly appears.

Strang.—But let us also consider it thus; for the object of our present enquiry is no trivial thing, but a very various and complicated one; it would seem indeed from what was before said not to be of the kind now stated, but something quite different.

Theæt.—How so?

Strang.—We divided, I think, the acquisitive art into hunting, and another kind carried on by way of exchange?

Theæt.—It was so.

Strang.—But of exchanges there are two sorts, one by way of gift, the other of purchase.

Theæt.—Yes.

STRANG.—And shall we also divide purchase into two kinds?

THEÆT.—How?

STRANG.—By distinguishing those exchanging their own productions from those exchanging the productions of others.

THEÆT.—Very well.

STRANG.—But of all exchange, is not that which takes place within the same city, constituting nearly half of the whole, called retail traffic?

THEÆT.—Yes.

STRANG.—And that which occurs in the way of purchase and sale between city and city is called wholesale or mercantile?

THEÆT.—Of course.

STRANG.—And observe, one kind of trade exchanges for money things for the use and nourishment of the body, another things for the use of the soul.

THEÆT.—How mean you?

STRANG.—That which concerns the soul escapes us, perhaps; the other kind we understand well enough.

THEÆT.—Yes.

STRANG.—Well then, may we not say that he who imports and furnishes the different kinds of ornamental culture, the arts of music, painting, wonder-working, and other aids of the soul, destined either for its amusement or instruction, deserves the name of trader or merchant, quite as much as the purveyor of meat and drink.

Theæt.—Very true.

Strang.—And does not the same name belong also to him who buys knowledge and sells it again from city to city?

Theæt.—Certainly.

Strang.—But of this traffic in commodities for the soul may not one part be justly styled display; while the other, though no less ridiculous than the former, must nevertheless, as a selling of learning, be called by some analogous name?

Theæt.—Certainly.

Strang.—Of this traffic in knowledge and learning, then, that part which concerns the arts generally must be called by one name, that which concerns virtue by another.

Theæt.—Very true.

Strang.—Dealing in arts and accomplishments is a sufficient designation of the one; for the other do you yourself devise a name.

Theæt.—What other name can we well give it but that of the Sophistical art which we are now seeking?

Strang.—No other, certainly! Now then let us recapitulate the heads of our second description of it, having the characteristics of acquisition, acquisition by exchange, commercially exchanging, trading,

trading in commodities concerning the soul, namely, in reasonings and knowledge, and trafficking in virtue.

THEÆT.—Very true.

STRANG.—Again, thirdly, if any one coming to establish himself in the city should propose to get his living by selling such stores of learning, partly purchased and partly fabricated by himself, you would give him no other name.

THEÆT.—Certainly.

STRANG.—That acquisitive art, then, which is carried on by traffic and exchange, whether the commodities sold are bought or self-produced, must in both cases, if dealing with commodities of learning, be termed Sophistical.

THEÆT.—Certainly; such is the necessary inference.

STRANG.—Let us also consider whether what we are now seeking is not allied to something like 225 the following:—Of the acquisitive art one part, you may recollect, we defined as contentious or competitive.

THEÆT.—True.

STRANG.—We may then, as usual, divide it into two sorts—the struggle of rivals, and the fight of foes.

THEÆT.—Well.

STRANG.—Of fighting, that kind which is carried on bodily between man and man may be termed violent; whereas strife carried on in words against words is controversy.

Theæt.—Yes.

Strang.—But controversies are of two sorts: those publicly held in continuous discourses on questions of just and unjust are legal pleadings; those privately conducted in the form of question and answer are called disputations.

Theæt.—Yes.

Strang.—But disputation, so far as it concerns business contracts, and is carried on carelessly and unartificially, though recognisable as a separate kind, has not obtained a distinct name in former time, nor shall it now from us.

Theæt.—Certainly; for it concerns only a variety of small trivialities.

Strang.—But the artificial kind, which treats generally the nature of justice and injustice and other matters, we are wont to call "eristic" or wrangling.

Theæt.—Yes.

Strang.—But of wrangling—one sort destroys wealth, the other increases it.

Theæt.—Very true.

Strang.—That which occurs to the neglect of our private affairs, to gratify the idle garrulity of the speaker, and often to the disgust of the hearers, may, I think, be called prosing or babbling.

THEÆT.—So it may, indeed.

STRANG.—And the kind opposed to this, which makes money out of private disputations, what would you term it?

THEÆT.—What answer can be given to such a question except that we have here a fourth characteristic of the wonderful being we are in search of, namely the Sophist?

STRANG.—It doubtless is that acquisitive race 226 which, practising the general art of wrangling and controversy, is specially distinguished by the private character of its contentions and their lucrative results.[1]

THEÆT.—Very true.

STRANG.—You see, then, how true it is that this is a various and very questionable animal—one not to be caught with the left hand, as the saying is.

THEÆT.—Nay; we must use both hands.

STRANG.—True; and let us do our best to do so, following up its footmarks, for instance, as follows: say, do we not sometimes employ household terms?

---

[1] The class of acquisitive artists leads to the identification of the Sophist as a practitioner in the way of arbitrary seizure,—as a hunter or fisher of men—a hunter for profit; while through another derivation from the same genus, through acquirers by consent, we come to exchangers—itinerant hawkers providing merchandise for the mind, the purveyors of accomplishments and sophists. Again, a reference to the class of acquirers without consent leads, through the subdivision contenders, to the specification of fighters or contenders in argument, public pleaders and private disputants; some wrangling as amateurs, others professionally; and here, too, we find the sophist.

THEÆT.—To which do you allude?

STRANG.—Expressions such as straining, filtering, sifting, sorting?[1]

THEÆT.—Of course.

STRANG.—Moreover, carding, weaving, combing, and many other expressions used in the arts.

THEÆT.—For what particular purpose of explanation do you select these instances?

STRANG.—All these instances denote division and separation.

THEÆT.—Yes.

STRANG.—Since, then, one operation pervades them all, we may apply one name to all.

THEÆT.—What name?

STRANG.—The discriminative art (Diacritike).

THEÆT.—Be it so.

STRANG.—Consider, now, if there be two sorts of this.

THEÆT.—You are rather too quick for me.

STRANG.—Of the divisions alluded to, some are of better from worse, some of like from like.

THEÆT.—So, indeed, it seems.

STRANG.—For one of these I have no name; but

---

[1] Another specification of the Sophist branches off here from one of the miscellaneous arts alluded to, namely those consisting in sifting or separating, one kind of which is purification, leading to the subdivision mental purification; this being indeed the proper task of the generic Sophist or genuine teacher;—the instrument for effecting it is the Elenchus,—the process of dialectial refutation, which however admits of being prostituted to purposes very inferior to its true and rightful aim of purification.

for that which leaves the good and rejects the bad, I have one.

THEÆT.—What is it?

STRANG.—All separation of this nature is called, I think, purification.

THEÆT.—So it is.

STRANG.—And are there not two sorts of purification?

THEÆT.—Yes, perhaps, if one had time to consider; but I don't at present see it.

STRANG.—The various kinds of bodily purification may be comprehended under one name.

THEÆT.—What are they?

STRANG.—In regard to animal bodies, the legitimate inward purifications of exercise and medicine; in regard to the outside, all that is effected by bathing; in the inanimate, all that is done by the fuller's art and by cosmetics, suggesting many minute specialities and ridiculous terms.

THEÆT.—Certainly.

STRANG.—Yes, Theætetus; but our method of enquiry cares little for differences of quality or utility in the particular kinds of purification cited as examples. For its aim is clear and definite ideas;[1] for this it endeavours to distinguish in all

[1] See Mr. Grote's excellent remarks—(Plato, vol. ii. p. 406)—on the tendency of prejudices of emotional sentiment to intrude prejudicially into philosophical enquiries;—no obstacle to the discovery of truth being more general or more pernicious than this.

arts that which is similar or dissimilar, treating all for its own particular purpose as being on the same footing in regard to dignity—none of them, indeed, as more despicable than another if only it can supply a useful analogy. For instance, it does not esteem the hunting pursued in a military campaign more really important than the hunting of vermin, but only a more ostentatious and pretentious sort of it. In reference to your question, it matters not by what name we denominate the various purifications of animate or inanimate bodies; only it should be one comprehending all, purifications of the soul excepted. Our sole object, at present, is to separate mental from other sorts of purification.

Theæt.—I understand, and admit two sorts: one relating to the body, the other to the soul.

Strang.—Very well. Now listen; try to divide the kind just alluded to into two parts.

Theæt.—Lead, and I will try to follow you in the division.

Strang.—Do we not reckon vice as differing from virtue in the soul?

Theæt.—Certainly.

Strang.—And purification was found to consist in leaving the one and expelling what is evil?

Theæt.—Of course.

Strang.—Any expulsion of depravity from the soul then may properly be termed purification?

THEÆT.—Certainly.

STRANG.—We may, I think, distinguish two kinds of mental depravity,—one analogous to bodily sickness, the other to bodily deformity.

THEÆT.—I don't follow.

STRANG.—Are not sickness and sedition identical things?

THEÆT. I don't quite see.

STRANG.—Is not sedition a corruption of something naturally allied, in consequence of some discord?

THEÆT.—Yes.

STRANG.—And is deformity anything but the repulsive appearance arising wherever harmony is absent?

THEÆT.—Nothing else.

STRANG.—Well then,—do we not see in the souls of the ill-conditioned, opinion at issue with desire, fortitude with pleasure, reason with pain, and indeed discord of all kinds?

THEÆT.—Certainly.

STRANG.—Nevertheless all these elements are naturally allied?

THEÆT.—Of course they are.

STRANG.—We may therefore aptly call vice a sedition and disease of the soul.

THEÆT.—Very truly so.

STRANG.—But when things having motion and a

certain end in view, fail in their efforts to reach it by being carried hither and thither by particular impulses, shall we say that the failure arises from internal harmony and congruity, or from incongruity?

THEÆT.—Evidently through incongruity.

STRANG.—But we are certain that all ignorance is contrary to the instincts of the soul.

THEÆT.—Quite so.

STRANG.—Ignorance, however, is only the error of a soul aiming at truth, but swerving from its course.

THEÆT.—Assuredly.

STRANG.—An ignorant soul must therefore be considered deformed and inharmonious?

THEÆT.—So it appears.

STRANG.—There are then two kinds of evil besetting it; one called by the many vice or depravity, and being most certainly a disease in it; the other ignorance; but this they will not allow to be the special vice of the soul.

THEÆT.—I must admit the truth of what I just now doubted, namely what you said about there being two kinds of vice in the soul; cowardice, intemperance, injustice, and faults of this description, must be allowed to be diseases; but the state of ignorance in its various phases is deformity.

STRANG.—But now, so far as the body is concerned, are there not two arts dealing with these two evils respectively?

THEÆT.—What are they?

STRANG.—Gymnastics for deformity, medicine for disease. 229

THEÆT.—'Tis so indeed.

STRANG.—To repress insolence, injustice, cowardice, etc., is not the best preservative that which punishes, namely law or justice?

THEÆT.—So it appears, to human estimation at least.

STRANG.—But for ignorance generally what remedy is there except instruction?

THEÆT.—None.

STRANG.—But now, consider; is there one kind of instruction only or several; and of many are not two of supreme importance? Reflect!

THEÆT.—Well. I am reflecting.

STRANG.—It seems to me that we shall best get an answer by considering whether ignorance does not admit a two-fold division, for so each of its divisions will ask its own special remedy.

THEÆT.—Do you see the way to a solution?

STRANG.—Yes. I do think I see a great and very dangerous kind of ignorance, which alone may well be considered equivalent to all its other forms.

THEÆT.—Which is it?

STRANG.—The fancying we know when we are in

fact ignorant; out of which mistake almost all our intellectual errors arise.

THEÆT.—True.

STRANG.—I think it is this sort of ignorance which has specially earned the name stupidity (αμαθια).

THEÆT.—Very true.

STRANG.—Which kind of instruction then shall we propose as a remedy for this?

THEÆT.—All other teaching may, I think, be called handicraft teaching;[1] the kind here particularly required is among us at Athens called education.

STRANG.—So it is, Theætetus, by nearly all the Greeks; but let us consider whether education be entirely homogeneous, or something admitting division.

THEÆT.—We must consider this.

STRANG.—It seems to me then to be susceptible of division,—of the teaching by means of discourse one way appears to me difficult, the other easier.

THEÆT.—Tell me which they are.

STRANG.—One is the respectable hereditary practice used of old, and even now, when a fault is committed, either in the way of angry reprimand or

[1] "The object of the education usually given to the poor in England is not to help them on, to inspire them with intelligence and energy— it is rather to teach them to do their duty in the state of life to which, as said in the Catechism, they have been called. First get your state or society, and then train individuals and classes to fit their proper niches in it."—*Saturday Review*, Nov. 23, 1867, p. 656.

mild reproval; all this may pass by the name of admonition.

THEÆT.—So it is.

STRANG.—But the other kind,—since some seem, after mature reflection, to have come to the conclusion that all ignorance is involuntary, and that no one esteeming himself wise would wish to learn the things which he thinks he already knows, and under any circumstances would benefit but little from the admonitory method—

THEÆT.—And they are right.

STRANG.—So they address themselves in another way to eradicate this opinion.

THEÆT.—How?

STRANG.—They question a man as to things about which he thinks he can speak when in reality he cannot. They expose the vacillating uncertainty of his opinions, placing the latter as summarised from the discourse side by side in clear contrast, so as to show their essential weakness and inconsistency. Seeing this, their authors get angry with themselves and at the same time more tolerant towards others; and in this way they become emancipated from strongly self-complacent and inveterate prejudices, an emancipation very pleasant to listen to and very salutary to the patient himself.[1]

[1] This will of course be recognised as a description of the method of the Elenchus as used by Socrates himself.

For as physicians consider that the body cannot properly profit by the nourishment given it, until obstructions have been removed, so these purifiers of the soul believe that it cannot make proper use of instruction until obstructive opinions have been expelled, and the patient, shamed by refutation, becomes intellectually pure and clear, thinking he knows what he really knows, and nothing more.

THEÆT.—This is a most excellent and wise proceeding.

STRANG.—For all these reasons, Theætetus, the Elenchus (criticism or argumentative refutation), appears to me the greatest and most effectual of all purifications, and that he who has not passed through this ordeal, even were he the great king himself, is impure, ignorant, and uncomely in the important matters most concerning his real happiness.

THEÆT.—Very true.

STRANG.—But now, what shall we call those using this art; for I fear to call them Sophists.

THEÆT.—Why so?

STRANG.—Lest we ascribe to them a higher honour than they deserve.

THEÆT.—Yet the description just given resembles something of the sort.

STRANG.—So does a wolf a dog, the wildest animal the tamest. But a prudent man will be cautious in making comparisons, for this is a very slippery and hazardous kind. Nevertheless let them pass as such; for, if we are sufficiently on our guard, there will, I apprehend, be no dispute about small differences.

THEÆT.—No, it is not likely.

STRANG.—Of the discriminative or separative art then, let us take the purifying; of purification generally the purification of the soul;. of this instruction, of instruction generally, education; and of education generally let that part which consists in refuting the false semblance of wisdom be called, for the reason now given, the noble art of the genuine or generic Sophist.

THEÆT.—So be .it. But I am at a loss now, in consequence of so much having been brought forward, what we are to say with confidence that the Sophist really is.

STRANG.—You may well be puzzled; yet even the Sophist himself will now probably feel not a little puzzled how to escape our analysis; since as the proverb says, it is not easy to escape all traps; let us then attack him now with all our might.

THEÆT.—Well.

STRANG.—Let us, however, first breathe awhile, considering with ourselves, while resting, the many various forms under which the Sophist has presented himself to us; first, I think, he was found to be a mercenary hunter of the young and rich?

THEÆT.—Yes.

STRANG.—Secondly, a kind of trafficker in instruction of the soul.

THEÆT.—Just so.

STRANG.—Thirdly, a retailer of these same commodities.

THEÆT.—Yes, and, fourthly, a seller of wares of this nature of his own manufacture.

STRANG.—Correctly recapitulated. I will now try to recall a fifth characteristic; in the department of contention he was defined as a wrestler with words, a professor of the art of wrangling.

THEÆT.—He was.

STRANG.—A sixth characteristic was left in some uncertainty; yet we allowed, though with some slight misgiving, that the Sophist purifies the soul from prejudices obstructive to real knowledge.

THEÆT.—So we did.

STRANG.—But do you not perceive that when a person appears conversant with a variety of things, while nominally professing only a single art, this appearance is not wholesome, the spectator not being able to see the common kind referred to by the various accomplishments of such artist, whence he is induced to give their possessor many names instead of one?[1]

[1] This refers to the perplexity just before expressed by Theætetus

THEÆT.—So it indeed seems.

STRANG.—Let us not then through indolence undergo the same sort of misconception in our enquiry, but let us recall to mind the various predicates assigned to the Sophist;—one particular trait seemed to me especially to mark him.

THEÆT.—Which?

STRANG.—Did we not describe him as a disputer or wrangler?

THEÆT.—Yes.

STRANG.—And also a teacher of this qualification to others?

THEÆT.—Of course.

STRANG.—Let us then consider about what things such persons undertake to qualify others to dispute; and suppose we begin our inquiry thus :—say, do they profess to do this in relation to divine things, which are non-apparent to the many?

THEÆT.—They are certainly said to do so.

STRANG.—And what of the conspicuous phenomena of earth and sky and things pertaining to these?

THEÆT.—The answer must be the same.

STRANG.—When in private conversation questions arise about generation and existence generally, do

(231c.), who feels confused by the many different characteristics of the Sophist as above described ; the only way of dissipating the obscurity is to consider well the specific nature of the subject, and in the man of many ostensible faculties and varieties of accomplishment to look to those general features and that common essence to which they all refer.

we not find them powerful in reply and able to make others equally so?

THEÆT.—Certainly.

STRANG.—But again in regard to the laws and political affairs, do they not undertake to give ability to argue about these also?

THEÆT.—Assuredly no one would converse with them if they did not promise this.[1]

STRANG.—In regard to the arts, all and singular, is it not published and laid down in writings, what replies are to be made to the professors of such arts?

THEÆT.—You seem to allude to the writings of Protagoras having to do with wrestling and other arts.

STRANG.—And many other similar writings also, my good friend; may we not then say in a word that the art of wrangling implies ability to argue about everything?

THEÆT.—It, indeed, seems to omit nothing.

STRANG.—But, in the name of heaven, boy, do you think this possible? Perhaps you youngsters see this matter more clearly than us old folks.

THEÆT.—What mean you? I don't quite understand the question.

---

[1] Mr. Grote, not being "sufficiently on his guard," as recommended at p. 231, disclaims the distinction here drawn between true and false teachers; he says that Plato, being unwilling to allow the Elenchus—the great Socratic accomplishment—to be shared by the Sophists, "finds or invents a subtle distinction to keep them off."—*Plato*, vol. ii. p. 410.

STRANG.—Whether it be possible for one man to understand all things?

THEÆT.—Happy, indeed, should we be if it were so!

STRANG.—How, then, can one who is unskilled say anything to the purpose in arguing with the skilled?

THEÆT.—He cannot.

STRANG.—In what, then, consists the marvel of the sophistical art?

THEÆT.—How shewn?

STRANG.—In the power they possess of making young people think that they themselves are wisest of all and on all subjects. For it is clear that if they neither answered correctly, nor seemed to their hearers to do so, or did not leave the discussion with increased reputation for cleverness, what you just now suggested hypothetically would be realised—none would choose to pay them or learn from them.

THEÆT.—Scarcely, indeed!

STRANG.—But as it is, they do choose to do so.

THEÆT.—Yes; very eagerly.

STRANG.—I presume, then, it is because they *appear* to be intelligently conversant with the matters upon which they dispute.

THEÆT.—Certainly.

STRANG.—And they dispute on all subjects?

THEÆT.—Yes.

STRANG.—They appear, then, wise in the eyes of their disciples on all subjects ?[1]

THEÆT.—Of course.

STRANG.—But not as being really so; for this was found to be impossible?

THEÆT.—Clearly.

STRANG.—So, then, the Sophist is found to profess a seeming universal wisdom, not a real?

THEÆT.—Certainly; and this appears to describe him exactly.

STRANG.—Suppose we take a still more evident illustration.

THEÆT.—What is it?

STRANG.—This—and consider well before answering.

THEÆT.—Well; say what.

STRANG.—Suppose any one were to profess to be able not merely to speak and to reply, but to make and do all things by one art.

---

[1] Old things reappear in new forms, and the present is little more than the past in altered costume. How striking, for instance, the resemblance between the ancient Sophist and the "serenely omniscient reviewer" of modern times, for whom nothing is too obscure or complicated, and who lectures the professors of the several sciences in the elementary terminology of their own departments! Mr. Grote (Plato, vol. ii. p. 432) remarks that in an age when "positive knowledge" was scanty, it was natural for a clever talker or writer to fancy he knew every thing; yet this seems equally easy in days superabounding with this same sort of knowledge, especially if the pretension be made before an audience having less knowledge than positiveness. The professor on the other hand unfortunately often loses in point of comprehensiveness what he gains in precision, and is apt to speak in a uniformly assured tone on matters with which he is ill-acquainted.

THEÆT.—How all?

STRANG.—You forthwith forget the prime point of the question;—you don't understand, it seems, what I mean by all?

THEÆT.—No.

STRANG.—I mean by all that which comprehends you and me, and, moreover, other things, both animal and vegetable.

THEÆT.—How say you?

STRANG.—Suppose one were to profess to be able to make you and me and all natural products?

THEÆT.—What kind of making mean you by this? Not that of a husbandman, I suppose; for the maker you spoke of is a maker of animals.

STRANG.—Yes; maker also of sea and land, of the heaven, of the gods, and of all things; one who, having made these things, disposes of each of them for a very small amount.

THEÆT.—You are jesting.

STRANG.—And pray, then, shall we not esteem it a jest that any one should profess to know all things, and to teach all for a small sum in a short space of time?

THEÆT.—Certainly we must.

STRANG.—Of jesting or sporting, now, is there any more agreeable or ingenious kind than imitation?

THEÆT.—None. In that one word you sum up a very large and most multifarious genus.

Strang.—He, then, who should profess to be able to make all things by one art, might, by forming homonymous imitations of things, for instance, by the art of painting, and by showing such painted images to silly little children at a distance, cheat them into a belief of his being able to make any of the things he chose.

Theæt.—Very likely.

Strang.—Well, then, in the case of word imitations by the art of language, is it not the same? Is it not possible, by means of discourses, so to impose on the ears of young people, who are still far from the truth of things, by exhibiting all sorts of wordy imagery to them, to make them believe that the things spoken are true, and that the speaker is universally wise and wisest of men?

Theæt.—Certainly, there may be such an art.

Strang.—And is it not inevitable, Theætetus, that the majority of such hearers, when, with advancing time and age they become more closely intimate with realities, and compelled by experience to see things as they are, should change their previous opinions, so that what appeared great before should now seem little, and that which was easy, difficult—in short, that all the phantastic notions so engendered by discourses should be entirely upset by being brought into contact with practical facts?

Theæt.—Yes, so far as I can judge. But I must

admit myself to be of the number of those who are still far remote from truth.

STRANG.—We, then, who are here present, will endeavour to bring you as near to it as possible without the painful teaching of experience. But now tell me about the Sophist;—is it agreed that he is a juggler or impostor, as being an imitator of reality, or do you really suppose he really possesses scientific knowledge of the things about which he professes to dispute?

THEÆT.—How can he? Surely it is clear from what has been said, that he is one of those occupied with child's play.[1]

STRANG.—One must then call him a mimic and a mountebank.

THEÆT.—Certainly.

STRANG.—Now, then, we must be careful not to let the quarry again give us the slip; for we have now pretty nearly enclosed him in a network of argument, from which he cannot escape.

THEÆT.—What network?

STRANG.—We have convicted him of being a certain kind of juggler.

THEÆT.—So it seems to me, too.

STRANG.—We must then at once search carefully

---

[1] Abundant instances of this might be cited from the language used by materialists confounding perceptions with realities, their so-called "facts" often being mere elementary conceptions or mental impressions.

the image-making art, and, invading its confines, seize the Sophist, if he await our coming, so as to deliver him up captive to the king[1] whose servants we are; or if he try to escape by any bye-path of the mimetic art, we must follow him up, continually dividing the department containing him, until he be caught; for neither he nor any other shall ever boast of being able to escape the method of those who can thus follow up the game both severally and generally.

THEÆT.—Well said, so let us do.

STRANG.—Following our former plan of subdivision I think I now see two kinds of imitative art; but am not yet able to discern in which of them the species now sought is to be found.

THEÆT.—Tell us first what two kinds you mean.

STRANG.—One is the assimilative art. This is when any one produces an imitation according to the true dimensions or proportions of the original in length, breadth, and thickness, adding colours suitable to the respective objects.

THEÆT.—But do not all imitators do the like?

STRANG.—Not those who paint or mould any great work. For you know that if they were to give the true and exact proportions of the beautiful, the upper portions would necessarily seem smaller, the lower larger, on account of their respective distance or nearness to the eye. So that here the artist,

---

[1] Reason, that is; Comp. the Menexenus, ch. x., p. 240ᵇ.

abandoning literal copying, tries to give not the real but the seeming and most agreeable proportions to his imitative work.

THEÆT.—Certainly.

STRANG.—May we not then call the one, as being copied, a faithful image or copy?

THEÆT.—Yes.

STRANG.—And the department of the imitative art concerned with this is called, as we have said, assimilative.

THEÆT.—It is so.

STRANG.—But what shall we term that which appears indeed from a fitting point of view to resemble the beautiful, but which, when seen by one able to form a just estimate of such matters, is not really like the thing it professes to be like? Must we not call it an appearance or phantasm, since it appears to be like, but is not?

THEÆT.—Certainly.

STRANG.—And is not this sort very common in painting and all imitative art?

THEÆT.—Of course.

STRANG.—The art, then, which produces a phantasm, but not a true image or copy, we may term phantastic?

THEÆT.—And rightly.

STRANG.—But I before doubted in which of the two kinds I should place the Sophist, and this doubt still continues: for he is truly a marvellous being, very difficult to understand thoroughly. You see how very adroitly and cleverly he has at this moment hid himself in a genus in which it is very hard to find him out.

THEÆT.—So it seems.

STRANG.—Does your assent proceed from knowledge and conviction, or has a certain rush of words hurried you into hasty assent through the mere habit of assenting?

THEÆT.—What mean you by the question?

STRANG.—Most certainly, my friend, we are engaged in a very arduous investigation. For that a thing should appear and be thought to be, yet not be, or that a man should assert certain things, yet not true things, all this is now, as it ever was, full of difficulty. It is indeed very difficult to see how a man can be said to affirm or suppose falsehood really to exist without being involved in a contradiction.[1]

THEÆT.—How so?

---

[1] The proposed distinction between faithful and supposititious imitation, or between the truly imitative and the phantastic art, leads to new perplexity, owing to the current quibble about the impossibility of predicating falsehood. For falschood is that which is not; how then can it be said to exist? This was an inference derived from the memorable dictum of Parmenides denying the real existence of all except that true existence which is recognised by reason. Now falsehood is mere non-entity; he who speaks necessarily affirms that something *is*, and he who says that which is says truth. Moreover non-entity has no predicates—for instance that of number; it cannot even be conceived or spoken, for the very predicates inconceivable and ineffable require the connecting copula "is," which was supposed to mean affirmation of existence. Hence it would seem as if Sophistry

Strang.—Because this would be equivalent to affirming non-entity to exist; since, otherwise it were impossible for falsehood to exist. The great Parmenides, my son, was always conjuring us both in prose and verse to this effect—

> "Never affirm that non-entities exist;
> But carefully guard your mind from this way of thinking."

Such was his testimony, and a little consideration of the subject will clearly prove its correctness. Suppose, then, we examine it a little?

Theæt.—I am quite at your disposal, and pray conduct the argument as may be most suitable; lead the way and I will follow.

Strang.—So be it then. And now tell me; do we ever venture to speak that which in no respect is?

Theæt.—Why not?

Strang.—Suppose that, not jestingly or for contention's sake, but in sober earnest, one had to answer as to how and in reference to what the phrase "non-entity" should be used, what think you would be the reply?

Theæt.—You ask a difficult and to me altogether insoluble question.

in the sense of false representation were impossible—so that it becomes necessary to qualify the saying of Parmenides by the consideration that non-entity—and consequently falsehood—may *be* or exist in a certain way. Here commences the famous discussion about existence, the foundation of faith and truth as contrasted with fallacious seeming, and thus forming the basis of the essential distinction between the philosopher and Sophist.

STRANG.—But this, at least, is clear that non-entity cannot be ascribed to any entity.

THEÆT.—How can it?

STRANG.—If, then, not to be ascribed to an entity, it cannot be ascribed to anything.

THEÆT.—No, indeed.

STRANG.—But it is evident that the word "something" is always applied to some entity; we cannot pronounce "something" nakedly as it were, and as wholly destitute of reality; is it not so?

THEÆT.—Impossible.

STRANG.—And do you admit that when we speak of something we necessarily mean some one thing?

THEÆT.—Yes.

STRANG.—You admit that "something" means one thing, "somethings" many?

THEÆT.—Of course.

STRANG.—And does it not follow that he who speaks of that which is not something necessarily speaks of nothing?

THEÆT.—Certainly.

STRANG.—Must it not further be allowed that one undertaking to speak of non-entity not only speaks of nothing, but does not even speak at all?

THEÆT.—This seemingly ends the difficulty.

STRANG.—Don't exult too soon, my good friend, for the difficulty is before us still, and, indeed, the primary and greatest difficulty of all, since it concerns the very essence of our argument.

THEÆT.—How? Explain yourself.

STRANG.—To any existing thing another thing may, you will allow, be added?

THEÆT.—Of course.

STRANG.—But can anything which is be added to that which is not?

THEÆT.—Impossible.

STRANG.—But the general attribute of number, does not this belong to (the category of) existing things?

THEÆT.—Yes, if indeed any other thing can be said to be.

STRANG.—We must not, then, attempt to ascribe number, either as plurality or unity to the non-existent.

THEÆT.—It would certainly be improper to do so, as the argument shows.

STRANG.—But how can any one speak or think of the non-existent, either as one or as many, apart from number?

THEÆT.—How, indeed!

STRANG.—When we speak of "non-existent things" do we not predicate number?[1]

THEÆT.—Of course.

STRANG.—And is not speaking of "the non-existent" the speaking of unity?

---

[1] The words "predicate," "category," etc., here used in translating, properly belongs to a later vocabulary.

THEÆT.—Clearly.

STRANG.—And yet we just now denied it to be just or right to add the existent to the non-existent.

THEÆT.—Very true.

STRANG.—You see, then, that it is impossible rightly to speak or think of the non-existent alone and by itself, it being unthinkable, unspeakable, unpronounceable, and irrational.

THEÆT.—Certainly.

STRANG.—Was I then wrong just now in saying I had still to state its greatest difficulty?

THEÆT.—How indeed can there be a greater difficulty than this?

STRANG.—Do you not perceive, my good friend, from what has been said, that he who undertakes to refute the non-existent is obliged, by the very nature of his subject, to contradict himself?

THEÆT.—How say you? explain more clearly.

STRANG.—It is vain to look to me for a clearer explanation. I before showed that neither unity nor plurality could be ascribed to the non-existent; now I speak of it as one; I say "the non-existent." Do you understand?

THEÆT.—Yes.

STRANG.—And yet just before I said it was unutterable, unpronounceable, irrational;—do you follow me?

THEÆT.—To a certain extent—yes.

STRANG.—Do I not contradict myself in trying to combine being with non-being?
THEÆT.—So it seems.
STRANG.—Did I not in fact attempt to make this combination when speaking of non-entity as a unity?
THEÆT.—Yes.
STRANG.—And while declaring it irrational and ineffable, I spoke of this ineffable non-entity as one?
THEÆT.—Certainly.
STRANG.—But I am assuming that in strictness we ought to speak of it neither as one, nor as many, nor indeed to name it at all; since by so doing we necessarily mention it as one.
THEÆT.—Assuredly.
STRANG.—Why then continue the exposition as from myself, being proved both before and now to be at fault and defeated in this question about non-entity; suppose, then, instead of looking for a solution of the problem from *my* answers, we pursue the enquiry through the medium of *yours*.
THEÆT.—How?
STRANG.—Come now, try with all the generous enthusiasm of youth, exerting yourself to the utmost, to say something correctly about non-entity, adding to it neither the predicate of existence nor that of number.
THEÆT.—Such an attempt would be very absurd in me, after witnessing your failure.

Strang.—If so we must both give it up and finally dismiss the argument; and until we chance upon some one able to do what we cannot, we must conclude that the Sophist has with unequalled knavery undertaken to pass where there is positively no outlet.[1]

Theæt.—So it clearly appears.

Strang.—If then we say he possesses a certain phantastic art, he will easily take advantage of that use of language to contradict us by asking what we mean by image when calling him an image-maker? We must therefore consider, Theætetus, what answer should be given to the fellow.[2]

Theæt.—We should of course advert to images reflected in water and in mirrors, also to painted, sculptured, and other similar imagery.

Strang.—It is evident, Theætetus, that you never saw a Sophist.

Theæt.—Why?

Strang.—Because, if you had, you would have found him to be blind or blinking.

Theæt.—How?

---

[1] The Sophists were inconsistent, because, according to their own showing, non-existence can have no predicates, and so cannot be talked of ; how then themselves dispute and talk about that which they allow to be non-existent and ineffable ?

[2] The Sophist having virtually refuted himself by attempting to argue about that which is no subject of thought or of reasoning, will next try to refute us by taking exception to our proposed definition of him as an image-maker, and asking what we mean by image? attempting to force us to the dilemma of calling it an entity or a non-entity.

STRANG.—If you made him your proposed answer about mirrors and sculpture, he would laugh in your face for talking to him as to one possessing eyes; he would ignore water, mirrors, and eye-sight generally, and restrict his interrogations to the logical inferences of your own admissions.[1]

THEÆT.—How should he do this?

STRANG.—He would require you to define an image, the one common idea running through the many particulars you have named. Speak then, and maintain your ground manfully.

THEÆT.—What, O stranger, should an image be but a sort of imitative other or counterpart of the true?

STRANG.—Do you mean by "other" another true thing or repetition, or how another?

THEÆT.—Not a true thing, but a resemblance.

STRANG.—Meaning by "true" that which really exists?

[1] The modern Sophist,—following, more especially in England, the materialistic tendencies of the age, will generally be found on the opposite side, disparaging the postulates of reason, and insisting on the authority of the senses. A good historical summary of the later phases of this controversy will be found in a paper by Dr. Rosenkranz in Hilgenfeld's Zeitschrift für Wiss. Theologie, vol. 7, pt. 3, p. 225,—and Professor Schilling's paper on Theories of the Nature of the Soul, Giessen, 1863. Also in J. H. Fichte's Anthropology, p. xviii. *note.* J. Bona Meyer's "Streit über Leib u. Seele," and Paul Janet on the "Materialism of the Day," translated by Masson (Williams and Norgate, 1867). In a critique of the last-named work Dr. Flügel pertinently remarks that materialism is not contradicted by merely substituting the word force instead of matter, if the forces be assumed to be uncaused and aboriginal. See Zeitschrift für Exacte. Philos. 7, p. 193.

THEÆT.—Certainly.

STRANG.—But that which is contrary to the true is, I suppose, the false?

THEÆT.—Of course.

STRANG.—When then you speak of a resemblance as not true, you mean, I presume, that it is non-existent?

THEÆT.—No; it does exist in a certain way.

STRANG.—But not truly, you say?

THEÆT.—No, only as a resemblance of the true.

STRANG. - The image of the real is then a really existing unreal thing?[1]

THEÆT.—There indeed seems to be some such sort of combination of non-entity with entity, and very strange it is.

STRANG.—Of course it is; see now, how, in consequence of this ambiguity, our many-headed Sophist has forced us unwillingly to admit that the non-existent does in a certain way exist.

THEÆT.—I see it well enough.

STRANG.—What now shall we define his art to be without ourselves falling into a self-contradiction?

THEÆT.—How mean you? What fear you?

STRANG.—If we say that he deals in phantasms and exercises a deceptive art, must we not infer that our souls, misled by his art, form false conceptions?

THEÆT.—Certainly; how can it be otherwise?

---

[1] Reading—'Οὐκ ὂν ἄρ' ὂυν ὄντως ἐστὶν ὄντος, etc.

STRANG.—But a false conception is one formed in contrariety to that which exists, is it not?

THEÆT.—Certainly.

STRANG.—You mean then that a false conception is a conception of the non-existent?

THEÆT.—Of course.

STRANG.—Does the falsehood consist in supposing that non-entities exist not, or that they somehow exist?

THEÆT.—In the latter supposition certainly, namely that non-entity somehow exists; there is no other room for falsehood.

STRANG.—But is it not possible to conceive that that which truly exists exists not?

THEÆT.—Yes.

STRANG.—And this too is false?

THEÆT.—Yes.

STRANG.—It will then be equally false to say that the existing exists not, and that the non-existent 241 exists?

THEÆT.—Assuredly, and I don't see how there can be any other kind of falsehood.

STRANG.—Scarcely; but this the Sophist will not admit. For how can any one of sound understanding be brought to admit that things just before allowed and granted are unspeakable, irrational, and incomprehensible? Do you fully enter, Theætetus, into the Sophist's meaning?

Theæt.—Yes : he will tell us we contradict ourselves, when venturing to speak of falsehoods as existing, either in opinion or discourse; that we are constantly obliged to unite entity to non-entity, after having just before admitted this to be of all things the most impossible.

Strang.—Correctly recapitulated. But it is high time to consider what to do with the Sophist. For you see how many ready contradictions and difficulties suggest themselves as soon as we try to track him out in that art of mountebank imposture in which we have placed him.

Theæt.—Yes, indeed.

Strang.—We have gone through only a few of them; but they are, in fact, infinite.

Theæt.—If so, it must be impossible to catch and refute him.

Strang.—What, then, shall we yield to fatigue and give it up?

Theæt.—I am for continuing the pursuit, even if we only catch the fellow by the skirt of his coat.

Strang.—You must, then, excuse shortcomings, and be satisfied if we drag him ever so little out of the strong fences of argument in which he intrenches himself?

Theæt.—Of course.

Strang.—And may I further make this request of you—namely, not to take me for a kind of parricide?

THEÆT.—How so?

STRANG.—It will be necessary for our defence to criticise the doctrine of father Parmenides to prove that non-entity may have a relative existence, and entity be said, in a certain sense, not to exist.

THEÆT.—Such, indeed, appears to be the task before us.

STRANG.—It is evident even to the blind, as the saying is; for how, while these matters are neither admitted nor refuted, can any one speak about false reasonings or opinions, whether as appearances, images, resemblances, or phantasms, or about any of the arts relating to them, without ridiculously contradicting himself?

THEÆT.—Very true.

STRANG.—Therefore we must now venture to attack our father's reasoning, or, if reluctant to do this, give up the matter altogether. 242

THEÆT.—By no means let any false delicacy stay us.

STRANG.—Well then, allow me to make one trifling request more. I just now said I felt considerable difficulty and misgiving as to the coming enquiry, and such indeed is my present feeling about it.

THEÆT.—You did so.[1]

STRANG.—I fear too I may appear to you half

[1] Sup. pp. 236, 239.

insane, through the many turns and changes inevitably occurring in the course of the argument; for your sake, however, I will attempt it to the best of my ability.

THEÆT.—Be assured, so far as I am concerned, there is no risk of your appearing to act improperly in advancing boldly to this task of negative demonstration.

STRANG.—Come, then, how shall we begin this perilous argument? We must needs methinks take this course; first, let us examine that which seems already familiar, that we may not hereafter feel confused by making inconsiderate concessions.

THEÆT.—Explain.

STRANG.—Parmenides seems to me to have taken it very easily in his discourses, and the same may be said of all who have hitherto attempted to define the nature of things in regard to quantity and quality.[1]

THEÆT.—How so?

STRANG.—They all appear to be, as it were, telling

[1] In order to understand the nature of non-entity, it becomes necessary to review the opinions entertained about existence or entity; whether, for instance, it be one or more of the so-called "elements," or something underlying and connecting these, or itself "the one" and "the whole," as supposed by the philosophers of Elea. But every whole is compounded of parts, whereas the one, strictly speaking, is not so; though certainly it may be called a whole in a certain sense, as sharing the property of totality; it could not exist at all unless it did so. Moreover that which becomes or is produced, is produced as a whole; so that to sever unity and entirety from things were to deny their origin and their very existence (pp. 242-246).

stories to children ; one saying that there are three elements or kinds of being, some of them at war with the others, or again in amity with them, marrying, bringing forth, and nourishing their progeny. Another, speaking of two elements, as moist and dry, or warm and cold, brings them together and marries them ; our school alone, namely that of Elea, commencing with Xenophanes and even earlier, speaks in its poetical lucubrations of all things as one. Other votaries of the Muse, Ionian or Sicilian,[1] thought it safer to combine the two theories ; to say that all things are both one and many, held together by love and hate. Of these the more firmly modulated strain taught how the separated elements are continually reunited ; while the softer, admitting this to be true in the universal, contended that in particulars the all is alternately one under the sway of Aphrodite, and then again many and at issue with itself. Whether in all this they or any of them spoke truly it were difficult, perhaps invidious under the circumstances, to question ; yet thus much at least may be said, that they who so curtly wound up their several theories evinced little regard for us their ordinary readers, caring little whether we follow them or not.

[1] "Ionian and Sicilian Muses," meaning Heraclitus and Empedocles. See Karsten's Empedocles ; also Seebeck on early Greek Philosophy, in the Zeitschrift für Exacte Philosophie, vol. vii. Heft 4, p. 357.

THEÆT.—What particular difficulty do you allude to?

STRANG.—By heaven, Theætetus, when they talk about two or many, or the one as being or becoming, or speak of the combinations and separations of warm and cold, are you able to understand them? When as a young man I first heard our present problem about non-entity discussed, I fancied I understood it thoroughly; but you see now how completely we are in the dark about it.

THEÆT.—Yes.

STRANG.—It is quite possible too that the case may be exactly similar in regard to entity; that while fancying we understand it perfectly we may be really as much at fault respecting it as about non-entity;—in short, that we are equally ignorant of both.

THEÆT.—Very likely.

STRANG.—And the same may also be said as to the other things mentioned above.[1]

THEÆT.—Certainly.

STRANG.—We will then, if you please, adjourn our consideration of the other things, and now concentrate our attention on the main and most important part of our subject.

THEÆT.—You doubtless allude to the problem of

---

[1] That is, the various aspects of the Sophist. Stallbaum gives a different and inconsistent explanation of the "things" alluded to.

entity or being; we must first enquire what is meant by those who speak of it.

STRANG.—Rightly apprehended, Theætetus; yet we must pursue the enquiry as if in presence of those whom we thus interrogate—Ho! ye who assert the All to consist of hot and cold, or any two elements of this nature,—what is it you mean when you affirm both of these severally and conjointly, to *exist;* what are we to understand by this predicate " existence?" is it a third element to be added to the other two? for in assigning to both the attribute of being you surely do not mean that both are or exist in the same manner? for in that case they would not be two, but one.

THEÆT.—True.

STRANG.—But still you call both entities?

THEÆT.—Perhaps.

STRANG.—Yet even so, my friend, we must say that the two are clearly one. 244

THEÆT.—Most true.

STRANG.—Since then we find ourselves at a loss, do you yourselves explain what it is you mean when speaking of being. For you evidently understood the matter long ago; we, on the contrary, before thought we understood, but now find a difficulty. Instruct us then first in this very thing, that we may not fancy we understand you, and afterwards find ourselves mistaken. In making this request of these and all others who assert the All to be more than one, say, boy, are we asking any more than is fair and reasonable ?

THEÆT.—Not at all.

STRANG.—Again, as to those who affirm all to be one, must we not try as far may be to find out what they too mean by being?[1]

THEÆT.—Certainly.

STRANG.—Let them, then, answer this: you say only the one is or exists; yes, they reply; I rejoin, do you call being anything?

THEÆT.—Of course it is.

STRANG.—Is it, then, the same as the one, or another name for it, or how?

THEÆT.—What, O, Stranger, will be their answer to this?

STRANG.—Clearly, Theætetus, it will not be very easy for those holding this hypothesis (*i.e.* of the identity of the two) to reply to the question now proposed, or, indeed, to any other.[2]

---

[1] Let not any one imagine that, now that we are arrived at the happy epoch of so-called positive philosophy, these problems as to the many and the one are definitely settled or obsolete; they subsisted throughout mediæval speculation in copious draughts from new Platonism and realistic scholasticism on one side, and nominalism and Italian peripateticism—leading down to modern empirical science on the other; they still subsist in the alternative of all-matter or all-mind bequeathed to modern times by Des Cartes, in the seemingly incommensurate aspects of nature as considered in its atomic forces or in its general laws.

[2] Simple unity admits no predication according to this argument; —to say "the one is," already signifies a duality of unity and being;—

THEÆT.—Why so?

STRANG.—Because it seems absurd to admit two names after having said there is only one thing.

THEÆT.—Very true,

STRANG.—Absurd too to admit that a name may exist by itself without a corresponding thing.

THEÆT.—How so?

STRANG.—He who proposes a name differing from a thing, speaks, in fact, of two things.

THEÆT.—Yes.

STRANG.—Even if he propose the name as one with the thing, he must admit it either to be the name of nothing, or else only the name of another name, not of another thing.

THEÆT.—It is so.

STRANG.—And the one, too, is the entity of unity only, not that of a mere name?[1]

THEÆT.—Of course.

STRANG.—Once more:—will they call the whole something different from the one existing, or the same with it?

and if, as said by Parmenides, being be a whole (without which supposition it could have no magnitude, or be at all) this implies parts, and consequently plurality. Yet unity, as well as plurality, belong to being: this is shown by the capacity of inter-communion existing among the ideas, without which predication, and consequently knowledge and discourse would again be impossible.

[1] This is Stallbaum's reading; another has—"The one too, being one name of one, this too were the mere entity of a name." Steinhart suggests that, ens being the main subject, the sentence should begin with καὶ τὸ ὄν γε, instead of τὸ ἕν γε,—in the sense, "Even ens (or being)—if a name of the one, would only be the name of a name."

THEÆT.—Of course they must mean it to be the same.

STRANG.—If, then, it be a whole, as described in the verse of Parmenides—

> "Like the bulk of a perfect sphere,
> Equally balanced everywhere from the centre,
> Having no greater size or weight on one side than the other"—

245 it follows that such an entity must have a middle and extremities, and consequently parts; is it not so?

THEÆT.—Yes.

STRANG.—Now, certainly, a thing having parts may have the affection of unity, or share in all its several parts the quality[1] of unity; in this sense an aggregate existence or whole may, doubtless, be one.

THEÆT.—Of course.

STRANG.—But it is impossible for that which has this secondary kind of unity to be itself the very one.

THEÆT.—Why so?

STRANG.—Because reason demands that that which is truly one should be absolutely and entirely without parts.

THEÆT.—Certainly.

STRANG.—But the divisible whole in question, being compounded of parts, does not agree with this.

THEÆT.—I see.

STRANG.—Is, then, being or the existent a whole

---

[1] πάθος.

and one in the secondary sense, as suffering or sharing the character of unity and entirety; or is it not to be called a whole at all?

THEÆT.—A perplexing alternative this!

STRANG.—Right! for the existent, as partaking in a secondary sense of unity, is not the same as the one, and the all must be more than one.

THEÆT.—Yes.

STRANG.—And if the existent be not a whole in the aforesaid sense of partaking of unity, but be itself the very whole, it will turn out to be less than itself.

THEÆT.—Certainly.

STRANG.—And being minus itself, will not be existent?

THEÆT.—Just so.

STRANG.—The all, again, seems more than the one, the existent and the whole having each obtained their proper nature apart from the other.

THEÆT.—Yes.

STRANG.—But if the whole exist not at all, the same inference must be made as to existence or entity; and moreover, not only it could not be, it could never have been produced.

THEÆT.—How so?

STRANG.—That which is produced is ever produced as a whole; so that it is impossible to speak of existence or generation unless the whole be placed among entities.

THEÆT.—Such appears to be the case.

STRANG.—Moreover, the non-whole could have no magnitude; for whatever it be, it must be the quantity of its being which constitutes it a whole.

THEÆT.—Of course.

STRANG.—A thousand other similar insoluble difficulties will be found to beset the path of him who maintains being to be two or only one.[1]

THEÆT.—So it appears from what has been advanced; each point is linked with another, entailing ever more and more obscurity on all that had gone before.

STRANG.—We are far from having gone through all the current philosophic subtleties about being and non-being; but let this suffice; and now let us advert to those treating the subject on a different footing,[2] that it may be on all hands evident that being is no easier to define than non-being.

THEÆT.—Yes, let us address ourselves to these too.

STRANG.—There really seems to be a sort of battle of giants among them in regard to the problem of being.

---

[1] The object has hitherto been to show the difficulties attaching to the numerical conception of being as many or as one; this being as hard to conceive in the case of entity as of non-entity. Plato now proceeds to criticise the theories of those dealing with being otherwise than numerically, specifying two classes of them, materialists and idealists or defenders of " Forms."

[2] Stalbaum renders "ἄλλως" by—"pinguius rem tractantes"— or coarsely handling the subject,—as if an antithesis to διακριβολογουμένους were meant.

THEÆT.—How so?

STRANG.—Some of them are for dragging everything down from heaven and the unseen world to earth, rudely clutching with their fingers trees and stones; laying their hands on these and the like, they stoutly maintain that alone to exist which can be pressed or touched, defining being as identical with body; and if any one talks of the existence of the incorporeal, they frown and refuse to have anything more to say to him.

THEÆT.—These are terrible fellows indeed; I have met with such ere now.

STRANG.—Their opponents very adroitly defend themselves out of the, resources of the supernal invisible world, insisting that certain incorporeal forms (ἔιδη) cognizable by intellect are the true existences; and breaking up or analysing what the others held to be body and truth in their discourses, they call it generation or becoming instead of being. Between these two parties, Theætetus, there has ever raged the fiercest antagonism.

THEÆT.—Surely.

STRANG.—We will then reckon with each party separately about existence.

THEÆT.—How is it to be managed?

STRANG.—With those who attribute existence to "ideas" or forms the task is easy; for they are of milder temper; those on the other hand who drag all things down to the corporeal, it is difficult, almost impossible to manage. The only way of treating them is, I think, this; we must in the first place try, if possible, to make them really and indeed better; failing in this we must make them so hypothetically in word and discourse, assuming their willingness to answer more fairly than is their wont. For that which is assented to by the good carries more weight with it than the opinions of inferior persons; however, it is not of them that we have to think so much as about truth.

THEÆT.—Certainly.

STRANG.—Summon then our hypothetically reformed respondents to the bar, and do you interpret their answers.

THEÆT.—So be it.

STRANG.—Let them say if they admit a mortal animal to be an existing thing.

THEÆT.—Of course they must.

STRANG.—And do they not admit this animal to consist of body and soul?[1]

THEÆT.—Certainly.

STRANG.—Do they reckon the soul among existing things?

THEÆT.—Yes.

---

[1] Plato here shows, in opposition to materialism, that there must needs be some existence other than that apparent to the senses; such as force, the power of initiation,—leading to the inference of the sole reality of spiritual being.

STRANG.—But do not souls differ? are there not just and unjust, wise and unwise souls?

THEÆT.—Of course.

STRANG.—And do not these differences arise in each instance from the possession and presence of each of these different qualities?

THEÆT.—Yes, they allow this too.

STRANG.—Since then justice, and prudence, and the other virtues with their contraries exist, as also the souls in which they exist, do they consider them as visible and tangible, or as all of them invisible?

THEÆT.—As nearly all invisible.

STRANG.—But have such things a body?

THEÆT.—To this question they do not give one uniform answer; the soul they suppose to have a certain body; but as to prudence and the other matters enquired about, they would neither venture to deny their belonging to the number of existing things, nor to say that they are bodies.

STRANG.—Clearly, Theætetus, these men are mending; for the genuine original and earth-born (materialist) would not shrink from either assertion, but would insist that whatever he cannot clutch and press with his fingers has no existence whatever.

THEÆT.—You express very nearly their real meaning.

STRANG.—We will, then, once more question them, since if they will but allow any thing, however small and unimportant, to possess existence independently of body it suffices. Let them, then, explain what it is they mean by the word existence used in both instances, what they intend it to designate as naturally given both in the incorporeal, and also in that which has a body. They may perhaps feel at a loss here; if so, try and find out whether they are disposed to receive and approve the proposition we are about to make as to the nature of being.

THEÆT.—State your proposition and we shall see.

STRANG.—It is this: I say that that which possesses power of any kind, either in the way of acting on some other thing or of being acted on by it, although it be ever so little and for the shortest time, all this really exists; in short, I define existence to be nothing else than power or force.[1]

---

[1] Mr. Mill in his review of Grote's Plato (Essays, vol. iii. p. 355) calls the above passage "a happy aperçu, a remarkable anticipation by Plato of the latest and best results of modern thought;"—it were truer to say that "modern thought,"—meaning of course the thought of the empirical philosophy of the present day, is beginning to admit, in its own sense, one half of Plato's theorem here stated, namely, so far as referring to the ultimate nature of corporeal existence; Mr. Mill's imperfect conception of its import is shown by what he immediately adds about "Forms not being, after all, the *only* real existences in Plato's estimation;" but such a separation of forms from force is far from being intended by Plato, who immediately proceeds to question the theory of ideas or forms *held by the preceding philosophy*, and to endow them with power, life, and motion, to show that the same active power which appears in the agency of living bodies is displayed also in the phenomena of cognition and of thought. (See Zeller's Gr. Philosophy, vol. ii. pt. 1, p. 437). In this and other Platonic passages (comp. Repub. 477c, and Phædo, 99c) may be recognised the basis of Aristotle's famous doctrine of Ενεργεια, or the immanent eternal life of the universe, never really resting, yet every

THEÆT.—Having themselves nothing better to propose at the moment, I may say that our respondents accept this.

STRANG.—Very well; let a possible alteration of opinion be reserved on both sides; for the present, so far as concerns these parties, let this be understood as mutually agreed.

THÆET.—Well.

STRANG.—Proceed we now to the others—namely, the friends of forms, and be you interpreter of their pretensions. Say, therefore, in your capacity of expositor, do you not distinguish (becoming or) generation as something differing and apart from being or existence?

THEÆT.—Yes.

STRANG.—Do you not also say that, by means of our bodies, we have communion with the nature of becoming, the object contemplated by the senses;

where meeting the eye as if resting in transient phenomenal varieties of matter and form, It may be useful to add here an explanation of the much debated word "Entelechy" in its relation to form,—the latter being phenomenal only, the former an attribute or attitude of ever-changing life; so that if the general theory be designated by the term "Energeia," then in the figure below, the interior factors will represent the vital play of Nature's reality, while the lateral ones, alone contemplated by materialists, are merely subjective and phenomenal—

NATURE OR ENERGEIA.

| Matter. | Dunamis or capability— the prius of movement. | Movement. | Entelechy— attainment or fulfilment. | Form. |

so that "Entelechy" means the living energy realising forms, not apparent forms.

and by means of our souls with that of true and real being, the object contemplated by reason ;—that which you hold to be ever unique and changeless, whereas generated being is ever changing?

THEÆT.—Such is the doctrine held by us.

STRANG.—But what mean you, my dear friends, by the phrase "having communion" in these two cases; is it not identical with the active and passive influence just now alluded to as exercised by power or force? Perhaps, Theætetus, you may not exactly comprehend the answers given to this, while I, being more accustomed to them, apprehend it better.

THEÆT.—What, then, do they say?

STRANG.—They don't agree with what we just now said in reference to being when dealing with the earth-born fellows; I mean, when considering it sufficient to define it as consisting in *power* to act or suffer, even to the smallest extent.

THEÆT.—Indeed!

STRANG.—They rejoin that generation partakes of the power to act and suffer, but that neither of these powers agree with the nature of being.

THEÆT.—Is the objection well founded?

STRANG.—We reply, we desire further to learn from them whether they allow that the soul knows, and that being is known?[1]

---

[1] Intelligence implies act or agency; as through our bodies we communicate with other bodies, so we do through our souls with forms

THEÆT.—They do agree to this?

STRANG.—Well, then, are not knowing and being known a sort of acting and suffering, or both; or is one an act, the other a suffering; or are we to suppose that neither has anything to do with either?

THEÆT.—Evidently, neither with either; were it otherwise, they should be contradicting what they just before admitted.

STRANG.—Yet, assuredly, if to know be a certain act, to be known must imply passivity or suffering, and then being, so far as it is a subject of knowledge, becomes also subject to passivity and movement, which had before been said to be impossible.

THEÆT.—Very true.

STRANG.—But more than this :—surely we shall

or ideas; the communication is effected through a power;—it consists in a mutual play of doing and suffering performed in the spiritual sphere. Mr. Grote (Plato, vol. ii. p. 439) holds the argument here aimed by Plato against a certain class of Idealists to amount to a "refutation of the Absolute," and indeed to be self-contradictory, as showing the "Forms" assumed to be absolute to exist only relatively to our intelligence. But Plato says nothing of the sort; on the contrary, he anticipates the logical cavil, here ascribed to the Formalists of Megara. Action and reaction, subject and object, it is urged, imply relativity and duality, and so they of course do in ordinary instances, but the Absolute νόησις includes both, and if we admit spiritual life at all, we must be prepared to allow inferences unacknowledged by materialistic logic. Aristotle indeed complains that the *life* of the Absolute is not made sufficiently prominent by his master; see Metaph. i. ch. 9, sec. 19—but then the mythical language elsewhere resorted to by Plato when appealing to an active principle in the shape of a Zeus or Demiurgus must be taken into account; moreover, it should be recollected that Plato's theory is *primarily* ontological, not dynamical, so that the consideration of the Ideas as forces is secondary and supplementary. See Zeller's Gr. Philosophy, vol. ii. pt. 1, p. 441.

not easily allow ourselves to be persuaded that movement, life, soul, understanding, do not appertain to (perfect or) absolute existence;[1] that it is lifeless and unconscious, a motionless stability, destitute of the sublime attributes of mind?

THEÆT.—This were, indeed, O Stranger, a miserable concession to make?

STRANG.—Yet if it have mind, it must have life, surely?

THEÆT.—Of course.

STRANG.—And if it possess both these, does it not possess them by virtue of a soul?

THEÆT.—How can it be otherwise?

STRANG.—And if it have mind and life and soul, can we imagine this living existence to stand for ever motionless?

THEÆT.—The supposition appears the extremest absurdity.

STRANG.—The moved and motion itself then must be allowed to share the nature of existence?

THEÆT.—Of course.

STRANG.—It follows then, Theætetus, that were being entirely motionless, no one could have any intelligence of any thing.

THEÆT.—Evidently.

STRANG.—And yet, were we to concede every thing to be borne about and moved, we should

---

[1] τῷ παντελῶς ὄντι.

be forced in consistency to draw the same inference?

THEÆT.—How so?

STRANG.—Can you conceive the unique, identical, and immutable to be without stability.[1]

THEÆT.—Certainly not.

STRANG.—But is any mental cognition or understanding of any thing possible without these characteristics?

THEÆT.—Certainly, all knowledge implies them.[2]

---

[1] Parmenides and his followers spoke of ideal being as the immutable One; later speculators, as Plato's friend Euclides and the Megarici, introduced number and variety into the conception, but not movement,—(πολλὰ ἔιδη ἀκίνητα); Plato assigns movement also to true existence, here chiefly on the ground that without it there could be no cognition; yet he also insists on the inference drawn in the "Theætetus," that for the same reason we must hypothetically retain for ideal reality the seemingly opposed attributes of constancy and stability : for what is science or knowledge but recognition and appropriation of the stable and permanent? Thus the Heraclitean and Parmenidean theories merge in a more comprehensive one. But the real existence so endowed by Plato with movement and life as well as number, is still, as with Parmenides, *separate* from phenomena ; so that his theory,—(ἰδέαι χωριστάι) stands intermediate between Parmenides and Aristotle.—It need scarcely be repeated that the old perplexity as to the one and the many still subsists ;—how to reconcile the principles of constancy and variability, the one order or reason of the universe with the infinite numbers of its elementary atomic constituents,—this must in all probability ever remain a problem to the finite intellect, to be approached only through the concurrently pursued study of nature and of itself.

[2] Mr. Grote insists on treating the Platonic Ideas not on the footing intended by Plato, but in the way of their apparent origination as mere logical generalisations, as subjective thoughts of a mind, instead of objective entities or energies constituting a mind; hence he not only infers the theory, as here propounded, to imply, as above stated, a refutation of the Absolute, but also to authorise the insertion of any fanciful monstrosity or arbitrary conception among Ideas (see his Plato, vol. ii. pp. 442-444) ; as if

THE SOPHIST.

Strang.—And assuredly we ought to contend with all our might against any one who, while obliterating belief in science, understanding, and reason, pretends to speak with assured certainty about anything whatever?

Theæt.—Certainly.

Strang.—Consequently no philosopher or friend of truth ought to accept the doctrine of the absolute immobility of the All, whether viewed as one or as many; nor, on the other hand, listen to those representing it as wholly in motion; but should rather, as children do when asked to choose, decide for both,—combining immobility with stability, whenever dealing with being and the All.

Theæt.—Very true.

Strang.—Well, then, have we not satisfactorily explained the problem of existence?

Theæt.—Quite so.

Strang.—Pooh, pooh, Theætetus! it seems to me that we are but just beginning to comprehend the difficulty of the enquiry.

Theæt.—What mean you by this?

Strang.—Do you not see, my dear friend, that we

Plato had foregone all requirement of verification, and as if the very object of the present dialogue were not to distinguish true conceptions from erroneous ones. The "confusion" alluded to is his own. Mr. Campbell, in his edition of the dialogue, notices how Plato "insists on hitting the real lines and veins of things," hence distinguishing between the artificial "μερος"—and the natural or essential division εἶδος.

are in the greatest ignorance respecting it, while fancying we are giving a satisfactory account?

THEÆT.—To me it appeared satisfactory, and I don't see how we are unconsciously so wide of the mark.

STRANG.—Consider well whether our present inferences would not justly leave us exposed to the same questions as those we lately addressed to the maintainers of "hot and cold."

THEÆT.—Which questions? Do me the favour to recall them.

STRANG.—Certainly; and I will endeavour to do so by interrogating you as I before did those others, so as to make some progress.

THEÆT.—Right!

STRANG.—Well, then, are not motion and rest contradictories?

THEÆT.—Of course.

STRANG.—Yet you maintain that both and each alike exist?

THEÆT.—Yes.

STRANG.—Admitting both and each to be moved when you say they exist?

THEÆT.—No.

STRANG.—You mean then that both exist in a state of rest?

THEÆT.—How can that be?

STRANG.—You must then be assuming some third condition of being comprehending both rest and motion, and so viewing them as partaking of the common property of being you say that "they are."

THEÆT.—We seem, in very truth, to be divining a third kind of being when asserting both rest and motion to be.

STRANG.—Rest and motion then combined do not constitute being; it must be something distinct from these.

THEÆT.—So it seems.

STRANG.—Consequently being in its own essential nature is neither at rest nor in motion.

THEÆT.—You almost hit it.

STRANG.—Which way then can we turn our thought in order to arrive at a certain inference in regard to being? It's assuredly no easy problem! If not moved, how can it be otherwise than still? If not still, how other than in motion? But being has just now appeared to us to repel or stand apart from both; is this possible?

THEÆT.—Quite impossible.

STRANG.—And we should, moreover, remember this, that when interrogated as to what the name of non-being should be referred to, we were utterly bewildered and at fault. Do you recollect?

THEÆT.—Of course.

STRANG.—And now are we not in equal perplexity about being?

THEÆT.—Nay, in more, if possible, in my opinion.

THE SOPHIST.

STRANG.—Let the problem then rest here awhile unsolved; and since being and non-being seem both of them to involve equal difficulty, we may hope that, in proportion as the one becomes darker or clearer, so too will the other; and should we fail in comprehending either, we shall thus be most appropriately pursuing our enquiry as best we may in regard to both.[1]

THEÆT.—Very well.

STRANG.—Suppose, then, we explain how one and the same thing comes to be called by many names.

THEÆT.—As how? Give an example.

STRANG.—To man, for instance, we assign various appellations derived from colour, magnitude, form, vices and virtues; in all which cases and many others we say not only that man exists, but that a good man exists, and so forth; and so too in the case of other things, we suppose a single thing, and then assign many names (or predicates) to it.

THEÆT.—True.

[1] The enquiry into being promises to be of use in clearing up the obscurities of non-being. The different ideas, forms, or varieties of being are, as already seen, capable of intermingling and entering into communion with each other, yet not indiscriminately so; some being mutually exclusive; others admitting intercommunion with few or with many, yet not with all, unless "being" itself be an exception. Now the proprieties of this intercommunion may be investigated, systematised, and reduced to the form of art;—as the art of grammar teaches the due arrangement of words, so the determination of ideas suited or unsuited to associate belongs to "dialectics," an art in some degree common both to true philosophers and Sophists; only the latter hide themselves in obscurities of falsehood or non-being, while the former are hard to distinguish for an opposite reason, namely owing to the dazzling radiance of being or truth (down to p. 254.)

STRANG.—Here methinks we have prepared a welcome treat for the young and also for late learners among the old: for any one can readily cavil at the proposition that the many are one and the one many, exultingly proclaiming that it is absurd to talk of a good man, good being solely good, and man man.[1] You often, I think, Theætetus, fall in with men addicting themselves to this kind of quibbling, sometimes even grave and elderly persons, who through the poverty of their intellectual stock-in-trade make much of such like things, and even esteem them to be the perfection of wise discovery.

THEÆT.—That is quite true.

STRANG.—Therefore, in order that our argument may meet all who have ever reasoned about existence, let the questions we are now about to put be supposed to be addressed to them as well as to our former respondents.

THEÆT.—What questions?

STRANG.—I will make three alternative propositions, and ask which of them you accept. First, is

---

[1] This quibble, derived from the strictly logical postulates of the school of Zeno, is ascribed to Antisthenes by Aristotle, Metaph. 5, ch. 29; also to the "late learners" Euthydemus and Dionysodorus in the dialogue named from the former, p. 272^b.; see Stalbaum's Introduction thereto, p. 37, and his note to the present passage. Also Zeller's Greek Philos. vol. i. p. 764. What the Sophists did was to show the impossibility of knowledge on the two current elementary assumptions drawn respectively from a one sided appeal to reason and experience, and the present was one of the fallacies by which the first logicians tried to subvert all logic. See Kuno Fischer's Logik, p. 28.

it impossible to conjoin being or other things with rest and motion and other things on the ground of their unmixed singleness and incapacity to share each other's nature; or secondly, are all things alike indiscriminately susceptible of intercommunion with all others; or finally, susceptible of some but not of all; which of these answers, Theætetus, are we to suppose they would adopt?

THEÆT.—I feel incompetent to answer on their behalf; pray be good enough yourself to consider what would follow from their answers in the several cases stated.

STRANG.—Very well; suppose first that there is no capacity in anything to associate or share the nature of anything else, have motion and rest no share in existence.

THEÆT.—Certainly not.

STRANG.—How? Can either of them be, if they have no share of being?

THEÆT.—No.

STRANG.—The admission then seems at once to overthrow the first supposition, both in the case of those who assert universal movement and those asserting universal rest; nay, all who consider things as maintaining a constant uniformity according to forms or ideas; for all these conjoin existence when affirming the real existence of movement and rest.

THEÆT.—Certainly.

STRANG.—Likewise, all those who at one time unite all things, at another separate them, whether uniting infinite elements in one, or dividing one into many finite or infinite elements and again recomposing them, whether alternately or continuously,—all these affirmations would mean nothing were there no conjunction.

THEÆT.—Right.

STRANG.—Besides, they would be most absurd reasoners if they allow nothing to be called different (*i.e.* to vary in its nature) through participation in something else.

THEÆT.—How so?

STRANG.—They have continually to employ the category of being, as well as that of division, differentiation, isolation, and others innumerable, which being absolutely obliged to use in connecting their discourses, they need no adversary for their refutation, since they bear about with them a domestic adversary, like the strange voice of the ventriloquist Eurycles,[1] internally thwarting them and recording their own refutation.

THEÆT.—A very apt and true parallel!

STRANG.—But what of the second supposition? Are we to allow to all things the capacity of combining alike with all?[2]

---

[1] See Aristophanes, in the Wasps, 1014, and Schol.
[2] This opinion seems to have been held by Euthydemus. See Cratylus, p. 386ᵈ. Zeller, *l. c.*

THEÆT.—This even I can refute.

STRANG.—How?

THEÆT.—Because on this supposition motion itself might be at rest, and rest in motion, if they communicated with each other.

STRANG.—It is certainly quite impossible that movement should stand still and rest be moved.

THEÆT.—Of course.

STRANG.—There remains then only the third supposition, for we had but these three alternatives,— either that all may join, or none, or that some may and some not.

THEÆT.—Certainly.

STRANG.—Well, the two first suppositions being dismissed, the third must in fairness be accepted.

THEÆT.—Evidently.

STRANG.—Some things being thus susceptible of association, others not, the case resembles that of letters, some of which fit together, others not. 253

THEÆT.—Just so.

STRANG.—The vowels especially are as a chain passing throughout, so that without one or other of them it is impossible to join any letters together.

THEÆT.—Certainly.

STRANG.—How, then, is it known which letters fit with others? Does it not require the dexterity of art to join them correctly?

THEÆT.—Yes.

STRANG.—What art?

THEÆT.—That of grammar.

STRANG.—And is it not the same in the case of low notes and high ones: the person possessing the art of discriminating notes capable of blending being a musician, whereas he who has it not is unmusical; and so of other arts?

THEÆT.—True.

STRANG.—But since it has been agreed that genera or kinds are susceptible of similar combinations, does it not follow that some sort of science must be needed in order effectually to demonstrate what kinds agree with others, and the reverse; also whether the combinations are universally continuous, so as to be susceptible of intermingling, and again, in cases of severance, whether there are kinds universally causing separation?

THEÆT.—Certainly there is need of science—indeed, the highest science.

STRANG.—What name then shall we give to this science? Can it be that we have unsuspectingly stumbled against the science of the free, and while seeking the Sophist have found the true philosopher?

THEÆT.—How mean you?

STRANG.—Is not the separating according to kinds, taking care not to combine or distinguish inaccurately, either by confounding the different or severing the identical, that which is meant by the art of dialectics?

THEÆT.—Yes.

STRANG.—He then who can do this will perceive clearly how one kind or idea pervades many several individual things, and also how many diverse ideas are externally comprehended in one; how, again, the one extending throughout the aggregated many is internally knit together, and how many ideas are sundered and entirely inconsistent with one another.[1] This is what is meant by knowing how to distinguish

---

[1] Of the four dialectical processes or operations here enumerated the two first denote the original discovery of the Ideas, or the analytical and synthetical ascertainment of them as given in things or nature; the two last the consequent affirmative and negative aspects of their internal correlation, their congruity or incongruity, or capacity of intercommunion with each other. The first concerns the formation of genera from several individuals; the second the analysis of the genus into its comprehended subkinds or species; (although the words ἔξωθεν περιεχομένας—may refer rather to the complex metaphysical import of the empirical individual than to the logical entirety or formal circumference of the genus); in the third we come to the application of these data in thought and predication,—either as regards congruity, owing to the permeation of one idea through the many treated as a conceptual whole; or incongruity, comprising the cases of exclusion and entire incompatibility. There will then be two instances of analysis and two of synthesis;—congruity, in the first is opposed to that of the third, so far as the phenomena are conceived as aggregate or several; incongruity too differs in the second and fourth, in the second seeming as if neutralised in the genus (or integer), whereas when contemplated abstractedly and by itself the incongruity is complete. See, however, Stalbaum's elaborate explanation, and Zeller's Gr. Philos., vol. ii. pt. 1, p. 390. Susemihl, Genetische Entwickelung der Platon. Philosophie, pt. 1, pp. 304, 305. On the contrast between the Eristic and Dialectic Arts—one trying to promote scepticism by harping on captious difference, the other pursuing knowledge by discovering bases of rational agreement, see Zeller, ibid. vol. i. p. 765, and Kuno Fischer's Logik, pp. 30, 34.

scientifically between kinds,—between those, I mean, which are capable of combination and those not so.

THEÆT.—Exactly.

STRANG.—But surely you will not attribute the true art of dialectics to any except to the true and genuine philosopher ?

THEÆT.—How, indeed, assign it to any other ?

STRANG.—Certainly we shall always find the philosopher conspicuous in this department: yet it is difficult to identify him exactly ; and the difficulty in his case and that of the Sophist is of a different sort.

THEÆT.—How so ?

STRANG.—The difficulty in the case of the Sophist consists in his ever running off into the darkness of non-entity, the subject of his habitual concern and occupation,—and so eluding observation through the surrounding obscurity.

THEÆT.—So it seems.

STRANG.—But the philosopher, ever intently studying the idea of true existence by means of reason, becomes difficult to follow through the brightness of the region inhabited by him ; for the mental eye of the many is unable to endure continuously the effulgence of the divine.

THEÆT.— The explanation here is correct as before.

STRANG.—Respecting the philosopher, we will, if

THE SOPHIST. 151

agreeable, treat more accurately hereafter;[1] as to the Sophist, it seems impossible to stop until we get a clear view of him.

THEÆT.—Well said.

STRANG.—Since then it is acknowledged that some genera are disposed to communion with each other, others not, and that some may have communion with a few, others with many, while others again are free to combine universally with all,[2]—I propose we follow up our course of reasoning by enquiring, not about all genera, lest we be confounded by their number, but selecting some of the most important,—first, what are the specific qualities of each, then what capacity they have of mutual intercommunion;—in order that, though we may not be able to comprehend thoroughly the nature of entity and non-entity, we may, at least, not be without some comprehension of them, so far as permitted by the plan of our present argument, if, indeed, we may in any way venture unscathed to say that non-enity exists.[3]

---

[1] Plato here seems to intimate an intention to describe the ideal philosopher in a separate dialogue. See below p. 254b, and above 217a. Also the Politicus, p. 257a.

[2] From the universality of space and time, and the impossibility of thinking of any thing apart from these, Kant supposed them to be mere forms of subjective thinking. And a similar misapprehension seems now imminent in regard to kinds or natural forms; being discovered to be more variable and evanescent than at first supposed, they are thought to be little more than a mere arbitrary nomenclature or convenience of classification.

[3] But now, what are these obscurities of non-being in which the Sophist is said to lurk? The argument proceeds to show, that as

THEÆT.—Such, indeed, must be our plan.

STRANG.—The most important forms or genera are those just mentioned—namely, existence itself, and rest and movement.

THEÆT.—Certainly.

STRANG.—And yet we agreed that two of these are mutually incongruous?

THEÆT.—No doubt.

STRANG.—But existence mingles with both; for both rest and movement exists.

THEÆT.—How not?

STRANG.—These, then, are three?

THEÆT.—Certainly.

STRANG.—Each different from the two others, but identical with itself!

THEÆT.—It is so.

STRANG.—But what is it we are now saying about difference and identity? Are these also two ideas or kinds,[1] differing from the others, although neces-

there are many forms or varieties of being, so non-being not only exists, but exists in infinite variety. Each idea *is not*, so far as it is not another. Difference, or "otherness," in short, runs through all ideas. And he who alleges unreal difference, and denies real difference or real being is a Sophist,—an asserter of falsehood or non-entity; although the falsehood represents nothing else, it represents itself, the Sophist being its impersonation. (Down to p. 259.)

[1] Is difference or otherness a mere abstraction, as some seem to suppose, or must it not rather be referred to a real principle in nature, in which variability unquestionably plays so large a part? Although the general spirit and many of the particular teachings of Plato are valid for all time, it certainly does not follow that equal validity belongs to his specific theory of ideas; Aristotle at all events refuted one side of it. Yet it may be questioned how far Bacon's

sarily ever mingling with them, so that we have now five existences before us for consideration instead of three? or do we unconsciously mean by "different" and "identical" one or other of the former?

THEÆT.—Perhaps we do.

STRANG.—But motion and rest are not the same as diversity and identity.

THEÆT.—How so?

STRANG.—That which we affirm of, or assign as an attribute to, both rest and motion indifferently cannot possibly be itself either rest or motion.

THEÆT.—Why?

STRANG.—Because if it were, motion would be rest, and rest motion; for in both cases the happening of one or other to either of the two will force the other to change its nature, as participating in its contrary.[1]

THEÆT.—Very true.

STRANG.—For both rest and motion partake the nature of identity and diversity.

---

notion of forms was essentially an advance on Plato's; he too of course treats them as belonging to the "Natura Naturans" or inner life of things; sometimes identifying them with "laws," as in the phrase "leges et determinationes actûs puri;" yet with the qualifying addition—"Quod in naturâ naturatâ lex, id in naturâ naturante idea dicitur."

[1] Identity and diversity applying equally to rest or motion, cannot be the same as rest or motion; for these are contraries, and it were no more correct to identify them with equivalents of these contraries than directly to confound themselves. Suppose, for instance, identity to be the *same* as rest, while predicable also of motion; then motion would necessarily become confounded with its contrary.

Theæt.—Yes.

Strang.—Let us not then call motion and diversity one, nor rest one with identity.

Theæt.—No.

Strang.—And are we to conceive existence and identity as one?

Theæt.—Possibly.

Strang.—But if existence and identity are the same, we shall again find ourselves compelled to identify rest and motion, since both rest and motion exist.

Theæt.—But this is impossible.

Strang.—Then it is impossible that existence and identity should be one.

Theæt.—So it seems.

Strang.—We must then consider identity as a fourth kind or "form" along with the others.

Theæt.—Certainly.

Strang.—And must we not make diversity a fifth? or shall we take both this and existence to be merely two names for one thing?

Theæt.—Possibly we may.

Strang.—Yet I think you will admit that of existences some are spoken of as absolute, some relative.

Theæt.—Yes.

Strang.—And is not diversity always relative?

Theæt.—Certainly.

Strang.—Not so unless existence and diversity be

thoroughly distinct; if diversity could be participant of both these, like being or existence, then there might be a kind of diversity which is not relative; but we have just seen that whatever is diverse must always be so relatively to something else.

THEÆT.—So it is.

STRANG.—Diversity then must be reckoned as a fifth in the list of our selected forms.

THEÆT.—Yes.

STRANG.—And we may say of it that it pervades all the others, for each differs from the other not through its own nature, but through participating the form of diversity.

THEÆT.—Certainly.

STRANG.—We may then thus recapitulate the nature of our five forms:—motion differs wholly from rest—it is not rest, yet partakes of being as existing; motion, again, differs from identity—it is not identity, yet still it is in one sense identical inasmuch as all things partake of identity; and this equivalency and non-equivalency of motion and identity must not be taken amiss; for in asserting both propositions we do not mean to assert them in the same sense; in the first case, we mean the sharing identity in regard to itself; in the second, we think of the same thing's participation in diversity, through which, parted from identity, it becomes not that but another, so as again to be rightly styled non-identical.

THEÆT.—Very well!

STRANG.—And if in any respect motion should partake of the nature of rest, it would not be absurd to speak of it as resting.

THEÆT.—Certainly, since we agree that of kinds or forms some have a tendency to mingle with one another, others not.

STRANG.—Indeed, we came to the demonstration of this before, shewing it to be naturally thus.

THEÆT.—Certainly.

STRANG.—Let us repeat then—motion differs from diversity, as it also differed from identity and from rest?

THEÆT.—Necessarily.

STRANG.—Yet in a certain sense it is not different, though different according to our present meaning?

THEÆT.—True.

STRANG.—Well, then, having divided it from three of our forms, shall we confound it with the fourth, after having agreed upon five several forms as subjects of enquiry?

THEÆT—How can the number possibly be less than that before shewn?

STRANG.—We may then boldly assert motion to differ from being?[1]

---

[1] Without mistaking the Platonic generalisations or forms for more than they are worth, it may be said that they not only supply an ingenious answer to the sophistical quibble at issue, but stand upon a true general hypothesis, countenanced by the best modern philosophy

THEÆT.—Most certainly.

STRANG.—Is not motion, then, actually an instance of non-being, although at the same time being, inasmuch as participating being?

THEÆT.—Clearly.

STRANG.—Of necessity, then, non-entity must exist both in regard to motion and all forms, since through-

—namely, that the products of nature are products of thought—a thought, to a certain extent, ascertainable and reproducible by the reconstructive efforts of the human soul. See Von Baer, Reden, vol. i. p. 275. The attempts to re-establish philosophic realism during the Italian Revival by Achillinus and others—(though Achillinus clearly saw the difference between natural and artificial generalisation),—seem to have been ineffectual until the Botanist Cesalpini began to collect and arrange results in his own department, and after a long interval, Linnæus, followed subsequently by Cuvier in his famous controversy with Geoffroi St. Hilaire, assumed species to be inalterably given, or nearly so, by original creative fiat. Lamarck, on the other hand, broached the theory of evolution, and the assumption of an original creation with unvarying types gradually gave way before the progress of geological and palæontological research. Then the problem was subjected to experiment, and Darwin showed the wide extent of possible variation through well-known agencies, until at last the reality of species seemed to melt away. But here the Heraclitean half truth needs to be supplemented by the Parmenidean. Though nature allow no absolute arrest or pause, unvarying constancy reigns in her underlying law or thought, which is not a mere blind force implicitly following the line of least resistance, but one inwardly self-determined in that of progressive excellence. (See Prof. Nägeli, "Begriff der Naturhistorischen Art," p. 29.) We are not, then, driven to suppose that natural forms or kinds are nothing but illusion or mechanical accident—that man exists only as a sum of connotation or subject of classification—that his rational are no more essential than his cooking qualities, or his having four incisors in each jaw, tusks solitary, and erect posture." Mr. Mill (Logic, vol. i. pp. 142, 145) complains of the absurdity of the notion of an *essence* of a thing, making it what it is, and causing it to have the various properties distinguishing its kind; no one, he says, can tell what this essence is; and certainly it is not to be confounded with the logical differentia or the label of a naturalist; yet he would not assert that any amount of external circumstance alone would suffice to produce a horse, were there not some inwardly determining power at work.

out all of them the nature of diversity distorts and suppresses their being, making each of them in a sense not to be; so that in this way we may correctly speak of all as not being, although at the same time being—namely, as partaking of being.

THEÆT.—So it appears.

STRANG.—In each of the forms, then, there is abundance of being, also an infinite quantity of non-being.[1]

THEÆT.—So, indeed, it seems.

STRANG.—Must we, then, not speak of being itself as differing from the other forms?

THEÆT.—Necessarily.

STRANG.—Being, too, then may be said relatively not to be in as many cases as there are other forms; for though considered as excluding each of these, it is in itself individual and one, its negations (or diversities) relatively to other forms of being are infinite.

THEÆT.—Almost, indeed.

STRANG.—These positions, then, should not be thought extravagant, since genera tend by their very nature to mutual communion; if any one disallow them, let him shew that we are wrong in the former steps of the argument, and so proceed to dispute what follows.

[1] In other words, much may be truly predicated of any thing; but the area of possible untrue predication is still more extensive. According to an old proverb (see Aristotle Eth. Nic, 2, 5) the way of rectitude was said to be one, that of error manifold.

THE SOPHIST. 159

THEÆT.—Your claim is just.

STRANG.—Let us also consider this, that when we speak of non-being, we do not predicate the contrary of being, but only diversity.

THEÆT.—How so?

STRANG.—When, for example, we speak of a thing as not great, do we seem to mean the small rather than the unequal (or the relatively small)?

THEÆT.—Certainly not.

STRANG.—Therefore when negation is said to imply contradiction, we shall not concede this, but only that the negative sign implies some diversity or exclusion of the after accompanying properties or predicates.[1]

THEÆT.—Very true.

STRANG.—Let us also, if you please, attend to this, that the nature of the diverse appears to me to be liable to subdivision to the same extent as science itself.

THEÆT.—How so?

[1] Mr. Grote seems to misapprehend Plato when stating him to make "non-ens as much a reality as ens" (p. 447), and to resolve *all* negation into affirmation of diversity (pp. 423, 455); ens being expressly stated by Plato to have absolute as well as relative significancy, whereas non-ens, in the sense of diversum, is always relative, and always, when otherwise perversely thought of or spoken, produces sophistry or falsehood; in regard to the negative, Plato may fairly claim to be allowed to attach his own meaning to the terms he uses; he is arguing against those who asserted negation of entity to be inconceivable and ineffable, which he too admits it to be if understood in the absolute sense; he therefore puts it aside in this sense, reserving only its relative significancy in the sense of diversum, as manifested in forms of false opinion and false proposition.

STRANG.—Science, too, is one, yet each of its several provinces has its own specific name. Hence the usual enumeration of many arts and sciences.

THEÆT.—Certainly.

STRANG.—And is not this equally the case with subdivisions of the diverse?

THEÆT.—Perhaps so; but say how.

STRANG.—Has not the beautiful a certain diversity opposed to it?

THEÆT.—Yes.

STRANG. Has this diversity a name, or is it nameless?

THEÆT.—It has a name; for what we call not beautiful is that which is diverse from the nature of the beautiful, and from that only.

STRANG.—But tell me, is not the not beautiful to be considered as existing, as being severed from, and also opposed to, a certain class of existences?

THEÆT.—Yes.

STRANG.—The existence of the non-beautiful is then an antithesis of being to being?

THEÆT.—True.

STRANG.—And according to our present reasoning has the beautiful more claim to be reckoned among existences than the non-beautiful?

THEÆT.—No.

STRANG.—Similarly we must say that the non-great exists equally with the great?

THEÆT.—Quite so.

STRANG.—The unjust too must in this view be placed on an equal footing with the just, inasmuch as one exists no less than the other?

THEÆT.—Of course.

STRANG.—It will also follow in other cases, that since the diverse has appeared to be among the number of existing natures, its several parts or subdivisions must likewise exist?

THEÆT.—Certainly.

STRANG.—It seems, then, that the opposition between a particular segment of the diverse and a segment of the existent is no less existent—if we may so say—than the existent itself; not in the sense of contradiction between the two, but only of diversity.

THEÆT.—Clearly so.

STRANG.—How shall we then name it?

THEÆT.—Evidently, it is the non-existent or non-entity which we have been looking for on the Sophist's account.

STRANG.—Non-entity then is no more deficient in regard to existence than other kinds of being, and we may now declare confidently that it possesses a nature of its own, like the great and the not great, the beautiful and not beautiful; so, too, non-being exists as non-being, a specific kind or form among the many kinds of being. Is there any reason, Theætetus, for distrusting this inference?

THEÆT.—None whatever.

STRANG.—Do you see, then, how we have done more than disobey the immediate prohibition of Parmenides?

THEÆT.—How so?

STRANG.—Because we have not only not abstained from enquiry as he directed, but have arrived at a positive result.

THEÆT.—How?

STRANG.—Parmenides says:—

> "Never venture to assert non-entity to exist,
> But carefully withdraw your mind from this enquiry"—

whereas we have not only shown that non-entity exists, but also how it exists—namely, its kind or form; for we have explained how the diverse exists and is distributed through all forms of correlated being; and have ventured to call that portion of it which is severally antithetical to each segment of being as constituting in the aggregate the true essence of non-entity.

THEÆT.—Your inferences, Stranger, appear to me altogether unexceptionable.

STRANG.—Let not, then, any one assert that we venture to speak of non-entity as existing in the sense of the contrary of entity; since long ago we gave up asserting the existence or rationality of any such contrary. But in regard to what has just been advanced as to the nature of non-entity, let it either be distinctly proved that we are wrong, or else let

THE SOPHIST. 163

our adversaries agree that the kinds of being and of diversity intermingle throughout,—that the diverse, by participating being, is or exists through such participation, yet not as identical with that in which it participates, but as something different, and being so different from being, is so far clearly non-being; on the other hand, that being, by participating diversity, becomes differentiated from all other kinds or forms; and as such is neither one of them in particular, nor all together, nor any except itself; so that incontestably being appears in a thousand ways as non-being; and all other forms, both individually and collectively, in many respects may be said to be, in many not to be.

THEÆT.—True.

STRANG.—And if anyone disputes these antitheses, let him reflect and produce something better; or if, seeing the difficulty, he amuses himself by cavilling this way and that, let him be assured that he only wastes his time, as our present arguments shew. For this last alternative is neither clever nor difficult;[1] whereas the former is not only difficult but glorious.

[1] Mr. Grote's objections to Plato's description of non-entity as the different are two;—first, that "since Ens includes all there can be nothing different from the whole of it;" secondly, that Plato is illogical in using the negative sign in the sense of difference only, not contrariety. To the first it may be said that if Ens be considered as a whole, the parts must differ from it as well as from other portions of the whole, as Jones differs not only from Brown and Robinson, but in still greater degree from the nation and from the universe; if, again, Ens be considered as dynamically absolute—

THEÆT.—Which former?

STRANG.—I mean that before stated, that allowing the possibility of these (inferences or antitheses) he should be able intelligently to follow each step in argument, and, whenever the diverse is alleged to be in a sense identical, or the identical diverse, to discriminate the special manner and relation predicated of each kind; while, on the other hand, arbitrarily to confound the several kinds, indiscriminately calling the identical different, the great small, the similar dissimilar, etc., and moreover to exult in making this confusion, this is no genuine mode of argument, but only the rash venture of one newly attempting the problem of being.

THEÆT.—Very true.

STRANG.—And moreover, my good friend, a constant effort to sever every thing from every thing is inharmonious and rude, the part of one quite untutored and unphilosophical.

THEÆT.—How so?

STRANG.—Because the complete severance of

---

the "natura naturans" of Spinoza, each of the modi and also their totality summed up in the "natura naturata" will also differ from it. Secondly, in regard to the so-called "graver error" of resolving negation of entity into affirmation of the different, negation properly meaning not difference only, but exclusion and contradiction, it has been already seen that Plato proceeds on another hypothesis; he nowhere says that *all* negation means affirmation of the different; the seeming negations indicating something mean *for him* the determinate and relative—"omnis determinatio est negatio;"—therefore, *some* negation may mean, not contradiction, but only determination.

every thing from every thing else amounts to complete suppression of all rational discourse; for it is through the mutual interlacement of ideas or forms that discourse becomes possible.

THEÆT.—True.

STRANG.—Consider now how opportunely we have fought the matter out with these men, and compelled them to admit that one kind mingles with another.[1]

THEÆT.—To what end?

STRANG.—In order to make it appear how discourse forms one of our existing genera. Were we deprived of it, first and foremost, we should be bereft of all philosophy; moreover, it is especially needful to come to an understanding about it at the present moment, since if compelled to relinquish it as an existing reality we could not utter a word more. And this, indeed, we should be, were it admitted that there can be no union of anything with anything.

---

[1] The aim of sophistry, understood in its practical form of Eristic art, was to parade and exaggerate the perplexities of thought and expression besetting the approaches to knowledge, with the view of discouraging the serious pursuit of it, by inducing the mind to rest satisfied with immediate utilities, and with employing against others those expedients of fallacious refutation by which it had stultified itself. To the paradoxes of thought which occurred to Zeno, and the mysteries of life and experience which perplexed Heraclitus and Protagoras, all the subtle ambiguities of language were afterwards superadded; and it cannot appear surprising that enormous moral as well as intellectual power should have been needed to carry even a few in the ancient world beyond the obstacles by which even now many vigorous intellects seem hopelessly arrested.

THEÆT.—In this you are right; but I don't see why we should at this particular moment have to come to an agreement as to the nature of discourse.

STRANG.—You will, perhaps, best learn by thus following the course of the argument. Non-being or non-entity was found to be one of the other forms or genera, spreading through all existence. Was it not?

THEÆT.—Yes.

STRANG.—We have then to enquire further whether it mingles with opinion and discourse.

THEÆT.—How so?

STRANG.—Because if it mingle not with these all language and opinion must be true; if on the contrary it can and does mingle, false opinion and false reasoning become possible; falsehood, in thought and speech, being, in fact, nothing more than thinking or saying the thing which is not.

THEÆT.—Very true.

STRANG.—And from falsehood follows deception.

THEÆT.—Yes.

STRANG.—And deception implies the prevalence of visionary and phantastic images.

THEÆT.—Of course.

STRANG.—But this was precisely the hiding-place to which we before[1] traced the Sophist—he all the time utterly denying even the possible existence of

[1] See above, p. 235ᵇ.

falsehood; for he said that no one could either think or speak non-entity, non-entity no way possessing any share of being.

THEÆT.—It was so.

STRANG.—But the contrary of this has been made evident, and will probably no longer be disputed;[1] but perhaps it may be pretended that some forms or genera partake of non-entity, others not, and that opinion and discourse are of the latter class. Hence the Sophist may say that the phantastic and image-making art do not exist at all; since if there be no union of opinion and discourse with non-entity, there can be no falsehood. Therefore we will consider the nature of discourse, opinion, and phantasy, in order, in the first place, to shew their communion with non-entity; and, on the basis of this showing, prove the existence of falsehood, and having proved the falsehood, bind the Sophist to it, if he be guilty; or else release and seek him in some other kind.

THEÆT.—Most true, O Stranger, appears to be what you said at the beginning, that the Sophist is a species difficult to hunt out. For he seems to be inexhaustible in resources of defence, and we have to fight our way through each of these fences before getting at himself. Scarcely had we got

---

[1] The general analysis of the Sophist's nature,—interrupted at p. 241,—is here resumed,—on the basis of the discovery of the indisputable actuality of non-entity, and as here shown, of falsehood, passing itself off as truth.

through the pretence that non-entity exists not, when we had to face another, and to shew that falsehood exists both in opinions and discourses; after this we shall, perhaps, find another, and another after that, and so on endlessly.

Strang.—He, Theætetus, who is able to make even a small advance, must be of good courage. For what would he, who in these circumstances desponds, do in another case in which he should make no advance or be driven back? Scarcely would such an one take the city, as the saying is. But now, since the obstacle you speak of is passed, the main fortress may be considered to be won—the rest is easier and less important.

Theæt.—Very well.

Strang.—First, then, let us consider opinion and discourse, in order to ascertain whether non-entity reaches them, or whether they are universally true and exempt from falsehood.[1]

Theæt.—Very well.

Strang.—Well, then, let us now consider words, as we before dealt with ideas and letters;[2] for this way seems to lie the object of our search.

[1] This seems like the demonstration of a truism; yet how often do mere plausibilities pass unimpeached and assume an air of infallibility when uttered by a popular authority, or read in a printed book! How often is language used rather as a means of concealing thought than of honestly expressing it! Authorities should be weighed, not worshipped, and extremes of scepticism and of submission are equally misleading.

[2] See p. 253ᵃ.

THE SOPHIST. 169

THEÆT.—What, then, is to be said respecting words?

STRANG.—Whether all words agree together[1] or none;[2] or whether some do and some not.

THEÆT.—Clearly the latter alternative is the truth.

STRANG.—You mean possibly that those which follow each other in a sentence or proposition agree, and that such as are unmeaning when placed consecutively disagree?

THEÆT.—Why so?

STRANG.—I allude to what I presume to be your meaning in your last given assent; for in fact there are two distinct sorts of words used in declarations about existence.

THEÆT.—Which are they?

STRANG.—Some called names, others predicates 262 or verbs.

THEÆT.—Describe them.

STRANG.—Declarations about actions are called verbs.

THEÆT.—Yes.

STRANG.—And the vocal signs affixed to the agents (or subjects) of those actions are names.

THEÆT.—Very true.

STRANG.—Names alone uttered consecutively do

[1] The opinion of Euthydemus. Zeller, Gr. Ph. 1, 764.
[2] That of Gorgias.

not form a discourse, neither do verbs spoken alone without names.

THEÆT.—I don't see this.

STRANG.—Clearly, then, you were thinking of something else when you just now assented to what, in effect, I am now saying,—namely, that such words alone spoken together do not make a discourse.

THEÆT.—As how?

STRANG.—For instance, "walks, runs, sleeps,". and so of other words denoting actions; no amount of these strung together would make a discourse.

THEÆT.—How indeed should it?

STRANG.—Again, if you say "lion, stag, horse,"— and so forth, no such series of words amounts to a discourse; for in neither case do the words say any thing, by attributing action or inaction to being or non-being; this occurs only when verbs are joined with names; each then fits the other, and discourse is produced in its first and simplest form.

THEÆT.—How mean you this?

STRANG.—As when one says—man learns—here is an instance of the shortest and most elementary speech.

THEÆT.—Yes.

STRANG.—For, then, by connecting verbs with nouns, he asserts something about the existing or becoming things which are or are about to be; not merely recounting names, but also transactions; hence we said that he not only names but speaks, and called the tissue of such connected speech discourse.

THEÆT.—Right.

STRANG.—Thus, then, as among things some fit together, others not, so too among vocal signs or words some disagree, while to those agreeing together we give the title of discourse.

THEÆT.—Very true.

STRANG.—Add also this trifling circumstance—that discourse, in order really to be, must be about something, not about nothing.

THEÆT.—Certainly.

STRANG.—Hence it must have a certain quality.

THEÆT.—Of course.

STRANG.—Now, then, let us look to ourselves and our own doings; I will frame a discourse, connecting a thing with an act by means of a noun and verb; do you tell me what the discourse is about.

THEÆT.—To the best of my power I will do so. 263

STRANG.—"Theætetus sits"—this discourse is no long one.

THEÆT.—Short enough!

STRANG.—You are now to say what it is about, and whom.

THEÆT.—About me and my act.

STRANG.—But how is it with the following—"Theætetus, with whom I am now talking, flies."

THEÆT.—This too can scarcely be said to be other than of and about me.

STRANG.—But we said that all discourse must have a certain quality?

THEÆT.—Yes.

STRANG.—Then what is the quality of each of the two foregoing propositions?

THEÆT.—One is false, the other true.

STRANG.—The true one affirms that which is respecting you, the false something other than what is?

THEÆT.—Certainly.

STRANG.—Stating the non-existent as if it existed?

THEÆT.—Yes.

STRANG.—An existence different from that truly existing about you; for we said before that much *is* about every individual, and that much *is* not?

THEÆT.—Yes.

STRANG.—Now the last uttered discourse about you must, according to the definition given, be necessarily one of the shortest?

THEÆT.—Such was our conclusion.

STRANG.—Also about something?

THEÆT.—So it is.

STRANG.—And if not about you it is about no one —or nothing.

THEÆT.—Of course.

STRANG.—But if about nothing it is not discourse

at all; since we showed that it is impossible for discourse to be about nothing?

THEÆT.—Very true.

STRANG.—When, then, in speaking of you the different is stated as identical and the the nonexistent as existent, it appears that such a tissue of nouns and verbs is really and truly a false discourse?

THEÆT.—Most certainly it is.

STRANG.—But how about thought, opinion, and appearance? Is it not clear that all these kinds are formed falsely as well as truly in our souls?

THEÆT.—How?

STRANG.—You will understand better by considering separately the specific nature of each;— are not thought and discourse the same, save that the former, being the soul's silent discourse (dialogos) within itself, has hence been called "Dianoia?"

THEÆT.—Certainly.

STRANG.—And its outpour thence through the lips in sound is called (λογος) speech or discourse?

THEÆT.—True.

STRANG.—And this so expressed in words we know to be either affirmation or denial?

THEÆT.—Certainly.

STRANG.—But when occurring silently within the soul in the form of thought, what name can you give it save that of opinion?

THEÆT.—None.

STRANG.—And when such a condition occurs not independently in the soul, but as a consequence of sensation, what name can you give it save that of phantasy or appearance?

THEÆT.—None other.

STRANG.—Since then discourse was shown to be of two qualities, namely, true or false, and since thought is the internal discourse of the soul terminating in opinion, while fantasy is a compound of sensation and opinion, it follows that of these correlatives of discourse some are sometimes false.

THEÆT.—Of course.

STRANG.—See now how false opinion and discourse have been far more easily and quickly discovered than we lately anticipated.[1]

THEÆT.—I perceive.

STRANG.—Let us then not despond as to what remains, and having so far pursued our discoveries let us recall our former several kinds and divisions.

THEÆT.—Which divisions?

STRANG.—We distinguished two kinds of the imitative art, the assimilative and the phantastic.[2]

THEÆT.—Yes.

STRANG.—And we then professed to be at a loss in which to place the Sophist.

THEÆT.—So it was.

[1] See above, 260, 261.
[2] One producing correct images, the other only plausible appearances. Above, p. 236.

STRANG.—And while thus doubting we became involved in still deeper obscurity in consequence of the all-controverting suggestion, that there can be no unveracious image, similitude, or phantasm whatever, falsehood being everywhere and always impossible.[1]

THEÆT.—True.

STRANG—But now, since it has been made evident that there may be both false discourse and false opinion, it follows that false imitations of real being may exist, and that hence a deceptive art may be produced.

THEÆT.—Certainly.

STRANG.—Also it was before agreed that the Sophist must belong to one or other of those two kinds?

THEÆT.—Yes.

STRANG.—Let us, then, again proceed to divide the given genus, and so adhering to the right hand segment continually follow the characteristics of the Sophist, until, having divested him of all that he has in common with others, we exhibit him in his proper and peculiar nature,—for our own edification in the first instance, and next for the benefit of those who by nature are most nearly allied to his mode of arguing.

[1] Comp. above pp. 225ᶜ, 232, and Zeller's Gr. Phil. i. 768. "Περὶ πάντων ἀμφισβητεῖν" was, it will be recollected, the chief mark of the Sophist.

THEÆT.—Very well.

STRANG.—Did we not at the outset distinguish the formative and acquisitive arts?

THEÆT.—Yes.

STRANG.—And under the head of acquisitive he appeared to be among hunters, wrestlers, traffickers, and others of the sort?

THEÆT.—Certainly.

STRANG.—But now, since the imitative art has caught him, it is clear that we must first make a twofold division also of the formative or creative; for imitation is a sort of forming, that is, of images, not of things themselves; is it not so?

THEÆT.—Yes.

STRANG.—Of the formative art, then, let there be two kinds, the divine and human.

THEÆT.—I don't quite see this.

STRANG.—The formative or creative art was, according to our former definitions,[1] any force or agency causing things not existing before to exist afterwards.

THEÆT.—I remember.

STRANG.—Well, then, shall we say of animals and plants, and all things growing from seeds or roots, or formed within the earth of a fusible or infusible nature, that these were brought from non-being into being by any other than a creating God?

---

[1] See p. 219b.

—or, borrowing the words and notions of the many, shall we suppose them to be casual spontaneous products of unreasoning nature, rather than of a divine cause acting with reason and divine science?

THEÆT.—It is inexperience, probably, which makes me hesitate between two opinions; looking, however, at the present moment to you, and supposing you to be so minded, I now hold them to originate from God.

STRANG.—Very well, Theætetus; if I thought that hereafter you would be one among differently minded persons, I would even now endeavour to persuade you to the contrary by cogent reasons; but, knowing your disposition and that you are of yourself, without any argument of mine, already tending the way to which you now incline, I omit this as taking up too much time; assuming, meanwhile, that the so-called products of nature are creations of divine art, as those formed by man out of these are of human, so that there will be two kinds of formative art, one human, one divine.

THEÆT.—Well.

STRANG.—Divide now each of these again into two, so that the whole of formative art may appear in four segments, two dependent on us, or human, two on the gods, or divine.

THEÆT.—Very well.

STRANG.—And since they are again divided transversely, let one segment of each of the former divisions be called "freely creative," of the other two "image creative."[1]

THEÆT.—Pray describe them.

STRANG.—Ourselves and other animals, and the elements, as fire, water, etc., out of which things arise, each of these products we recognize as the very work of God, do we not?

THEÆT.—Yes.

STRANG.—And the accompanying images of these, not their very selves, these too are formations of divine art, are they not?

THEÆT.—What are you alluding to?

STRANG.—All sleeping and waking images that are called natural, such as dreams, shadows produced by intercepted light,[2] also the images reflected from smooth bright surfaces, where a confluence of original and derived light exhibits the ordinary appearance reversed.

THEÆT.—These two, then, are products of divine

[1] As thus—

Divine Free Creative.	Human Free Creative.
Divine Imagery.	Human Imagery.

[2] Or—shadow caused by the mingling of darkness with light; as *e.g.* in cases of twilight or eclipse, or even in the way of optical illusion as described by Brewster, Letters on Natural Magic, p. 21.

art, the thing itself, and its accompanying image or shadow.

STRANG.—But what of human art? Shall we not say that it too has a double function, one producing things, *e.g.* a house by the builder's art, the other, the painter's art for instance, producing a sort of waking dream?

THEÆT.—Certainly.

STRANG.—So that of these two products of human formative art the one may be called freely creative or autopoetic, the other imitative or image creative.

THEÆT.—I see now, and assume two kinds of formative art under two separate heads; human and divine according to one division, according to the other true existence and fictitious or simulative.

STRANG.—It should be also remembered that of the image-making art there were to be two kinds, the assimilative and phantastic, at least if it turned out that falsehood really is, as one among things existing.

THEÆT.—So it was agreed.

STRANG.—Well, such having proved to be the case, we may now assume these two, and then again divide the phantastic art into two kinds.

THEÆT.—How?

STRANG.—The one produced by means of instruments, the other where the appearance-producing artist is himself the instrument of his work.

THEÆT.—What mean you?

STRANG.—When any one in his own person counterfeits your person or voice, this aspect of phantastic art may, I presume, be called mimicry?

THEÆT.—Yes.

STRANG.—Let this name, then, be awarded to it as a distinctive appellation; the remaining portion it were more easy and agreeable to omit, leaving it to some one else to summarise and find a fitting name for it.

THEÆT.—So be it.

STRANG.—But mimicry too, Theætetus, should be treated as twofold; some mimics practice their art knowingly, others not; and what difference can be greater than that of knowledge and ignorance?

THEÆT.—None.

STRANG.—The instance just adduced was one of knowing mimicry; for only one knowing you and your appearance could imitate it.

THEÆT.—Of course.

STRANG.—But how of the form of justice and of virtue generally, do not many, destitute of knowledge and having only seeming or opinion, strive with all their might to counterfeit the semblances of virtue, imitating it as much as possible in act and word?

THEÆT.—Very many indeed.

STRANG.—Do they fail in their efforts to appear what they are not?

THEÆT.—Quite the contrary.

STRANG. — Such ignorant mimics, I presume, must be held to be quite different from the others, who know what they imitate?[1]

THEÆT.—Yes.

STRANG.—Whence, then, shall we get a suitable name for each? Evidently it is difficult, because former thinkers entertained a groundless prejudice against special and generic distinctions, so that none attempted to make them; and hence a dearth of appropriate names. Nevertheless, however rash the attempt, we will venture to call the mimicry or imitation resting on opinion only—" doxomimetic,"—that based on science " scientific."

THEÆT.—Very well.

STRANG.—One of these will suffice for our present purpose;—for the Sophist is an imitator or mimic, but not with knowledge.

THEÆT.—Certainly.

STRANG.—Let us, then, test the doxomimic like steel, whether he be sound or have a flaw in him.

THEÆT.—Apply your test.

STRANG.—A flaw he certainly has, and that a

[1] Mimics or imitators are of two kinds—the knowing and the ignorant. Of the latter—the class dealing with only fancy or opinion, are again of two sorts—those unconsciously mistaking their ignorant opinions for knowledge, and those acting consciously and insincerely in so doing, whom from their boisterous and obtrusive demeanour we may suspect to be purposely pretending to a knowledge which they do not possess.

large one. One among the number of such is simple, fancying he knows what really he only opines; but the other sort by his elaborate logical evolutions creates infinite terror and suspicion in the minds of his hearers, lest he prove to be ignorant of what he pretends before the multitude to know.

THEÆT.—There are indeed these two sorts.

STRANG.—Suppose, then, we call one the simple mimic, the other the insincere or ironical?

THEÆT.—Very well.

STRANG.—And of this last is there one kind or two?

THEÆT.—That is for you to consider.

STRANG.—I do, and seem to see two sorts; one able to play the ironical mimic publicly before a numerous audience in long winded harangues, another who in short private conversations drives the interlocutor to a self-contradiction.

THEÆT.—Most true.

STRANG.—What, then, shall we term the lengthy speaker, a statesman or a mob-orator?

THEÆT.—A mob-orator.

STRANG.—And what the other; a wise man or a Sophist?

THEÆT.—A wise man (or true philosopher) we cannot call him, having already supposed him to be ignorant; but as an imitator of the wise (sophos) it is fit that he should have some analogous designation; and now methinks I see pretty plainly that it is he whom we must address as the real and genuine Sophist.

STRANG.—Shall we, then, as before, summarise the constituent elements comprehended under this title, recapitulating the whole backwards from the end up to the beginning?

THEÆT.—Agreed.

STRANG.—Whoever, singling out that portion of the doxomimetic art, or art of fictitious imitation founded on mere opinion, which with ironical insincerity drives interlocutors to a self-contradiction,—derived from the race of phantastic human image-makers playing the charlatan with words,—whoever, I say, shall speak of the genuine Sophist as coming of this blood and lineage, will, in my opinion, most truly describe him.

THE END.

STEPHEN AUSTIN, PRINTER, HERTFORD.

www.ingramcontent.com/pod-product-compliance
Lightning Source LLC
Chambersburg PA
CBHW032143160426
43197CB00008B/756